DESERT MIRAGE

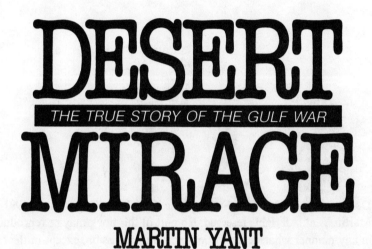

DESERT
THE TRUE STORY OF THE GULF WAR
MIRAGE

MARTIN YANT

PROMETHEUS BOOKS
BUFFALO, NEW YORK

95 94 93 92 91   5 4 3 2

Library of Congress Catalog Card Number 91-61600

ISBN 0-87975-678-0

Printed in the United States of America on acid-free paper.

For the courageous journalists who fought—and, in the case of photographer Gad Gross, died—for the true story of the Persian Gulf War.

All warfare is based on deception.
—Chinese philosopher Sun-tzu, 490 B.C.

The first casualty when war comes is truth.
—Senator Hiram Johnson, 1917

Contents

Acknowledgments

How can a journalist in America's heartland write a book purporting to be the true story of the Persian Gulf War?

Because, in the information age, it could be done almost anywhere by almost anyone who, with the aid of a few Washington contacts, took the time to analyze and synthesize the massive amounts of data on the conflict filed by thousands of journalists around the globe.

As Michael Massing noted in the May/June 1991 issue of *Columbia Journalism Review:* "To get at the real story in the gulf, reporters did not have to travel to the front. They did not even have to travel to Saudi Arabia. Most of the information they needed was available in Washington. All that was required was an independent mind willing to dig into it. In short, this war needed fewer David Halberstams and more I.F. Stones."

I wouldn't for a minute pretend to be an I.F. Stone. But the late master of paper-trail journalism, who preached that all the information a journalist needed was on the record somewhere, has long been a hero of mine.

Stone's philosophy is even more relevant in this era of the instant communication of immense amounts of information by dedicated journalists around the world.

That was certainly the case in the Gulf War, and I owe a debt of gratitude to all of those who covered this most-covered of wars. But certain news organizations and individuals are worthy of special mention.

Unlike the news coverage of the three major networks, CNN's—particularly in the war's early stages—was stellar. Even when the news anchors and correspondents at home fell prey to the jingoistic coverage to which the commercial networks had long ago succumbed, CNN continued to provide vital insights. This was particularly true of Peter Arnett, who did an outstanding job under trying circumstances in Baghdad.

As the main news source for daily newspapers, the Associated Press performed admirably by providing an overwhelming amount of material with dispatch.

But much of the most insightful reporting often came from newspaper correspondents who left the generally uninformative military briefings to strike out on their own. The staffs of the *Washington Post,* the *New York Times* and *Los Angeles Times* all excelled at covering the war from a variety of vantage points. (The outstanding reporting by Mark Fineman of the *Los Angeles Times* was a particular point of pride for me, for I gave him his first job—as a suburban reporter in Chicago—and quickly realized he was headed for bigger and better things.)

On the home front, *Newsday's* Washington bureau and its outstanding columnists—especially Sydney Schanberg—deserve special mention. So does the *Chicago Tribune* in general and columnist Mike Royko in particular. In his inimitable, blunt, incisive style, Royko picked apart President Bush's defense of the war much like Joe Montana picks apart an opponent's goal-line defense. The *St. Petersburg Times* also covered the war from the home front with verve and originality.

Several weekly publications also stood out in their coverage.

The remarkable reporting of Milton Viorst for the *New Yorker* was absolutely essential to a full understanding of the Machiavellian machinations behind the conflict. So was the insight—much of it uncannily prophetic—of *The Nation,* which more than lived up to its proud 125-year tradition of provocative and courageous commentary. The much-younger but equally perceptive *In These Times* also added a critical point of view, as did the *Village Voice.*

Closer to home, I am genuinely indebted to the following of my former colleagues at the *Columbus Dispatch:* Tim Feran for the wealth of insightful stories he brought to my attention and his expert editing suggestions; Barbara Carmen for her suggestion of the book's title as well as for her encouragement; Phil Rudell for his always-professional insights and editing advice; Sam Gruber for providing essential background material; and Lisa Reuter-May, Dick Carson, Mary Ann Edwards, and Diana Lockwood.

As usual, the people at Prometheus Books—especially Bob Basil, Lorraine Baranski, Elizabeth Gehrman, Mark Hall, Lynette Nisbet, Mike Powers, Kathleen Sarazin, and Dan Wasinger—went out of their way to be helpful.

Finally, I'd like to thank my daughter, Heidi Marie Yant, for her research assistance, my good friends Amy and Dave House, whose home became an oasis of calm during Desert Storm; and Pamela Ellinger-Dixon, for her wise words of hope in a time, for me at least, of despair.

Martin Yant
Columbus, Ohio
June 8, 1991

Foreword
by John Glenn

I first met Marty Yant back in 1978 when I was a freshman senator and he was the newly minted editor of the Mansfield (Ohio) *News Journal.* By 1981, Marty had joined the *Columbus Dispatch,* where he quickly rose to become a member of the editorial board, editor of the Op-Ed page, and a twice-weekly columnist. And whether as editor, columnist, or author, I've always found Marty Yant to be a journalist's journalist: a craftsman of meticulous research, insightful analysis, and unflinching conclusions.

Desert Mirage is Marty's second book—and it surely is not a book that will please everyone. But Marty doesn't write with that purpose in mind. His books challenge the conventional wisdom. They make us question some of our most basic assumptions. And they force us to take a more secular look at many of our most sacred cows. In other words, Marty Yant makes us think—and this book is certainly no exception. But whether you agree or disagree with Marty's conclusions or his point of view (and I have

---

John Glenn is a United States senator from Ohio.

done a little of each over the years) his work is always impressive—and always worth reading.

In the afterglow of our nation's spectacular military victory in the war against Iraq, it is difficult and even painful to consider some of the possibilities *Desert Mirage* raises. But for over two-hundred years, America has fought for freedom by battling for truth. And I think we can all agree that it would do our nation little good in the long run to win a war—and lose the real battle. Perhaps books like this one are the best insurance we have that that will never happen.

Introduction

The Persian Gulf War was undoubtedly the most watched war in history. But it also was one of the least understood. No wonder.

It was a war in which truth was not only the first casualty but its last concern, as media manipulation and censorship took new and sinister forms.

It was a war of deception in which plain words became elaborate euphemisms and respected reporters were called disloyal dupes.

It was a war in which fact became fiction and fiction became fact.

It was a war in which illusion about U.S. motives became reality and reality became illusion.

It was a war in which "spin control" became conventional wisdom and conventional wisdom became unconventional ignorance.

It was a war in which the recent past became ancient history and ancient history became irrelevant triviality.

It was a war in which recent allies like the brutal Saddam Hussein became enemies, and recent enemies like the brutal Hafez Assad became allies.

It was, finally, a war in which, to some, victory became defeat and defeat became victory.

Such ironies and hypocrisies are not new to war. As the Prussian military strategist Karl von Clausewitz said long ago, "War has its own language, but not its own logic."

But the Persian Gulf War seemed to raise the traditional war of words between enemies to new levels of intensity. From Baghdad, phrases like, "the satanic intentions of the White House," and, "we will make them swim in their own blood" ignited and inflamed, while Washington's accusations that Saddam Hussein was "worse than Hitler" and was "going to get his ass kicked" prodded and provoked.

Incendiary language, euphemisms, and censorship might be expected from a dictator like Iraq's Saddam Hussein, whose August 2, 1990, occupation of Kuwait sparked the conflagration. But they are not supposed to happen in the United States. Neither were President Bush's masterful manipulations and deceptions, which obfuscated several crucial points:

• Hussein had invaded Kuwait in response to several provocative Kuwaiti policies that Hussein had labeled "economic warfare" for several months. Among them were Kuwait's increasingly aggressive incursions into a buffer zone that had been temporarily established between the two nations until their longstanding border dispute could be resolved; the emirate's theft of Iraqi oil, with which it was flooding the world market and driving prices to devastating lows; and Kuwait's refusal to wipe off the books money it had given to Iraq out of the huge windfall it had reaped by supplying Iraq's oil customers during Iraq's war with Iran— which was waged partially at Kuwait's urging.

• By accident or by design, the United States may have helped to create the crisis when a Mideast expert often used as an intermediary by Bush reportedly encouraged Iraq to pursue an aggressive policy to obtain higher oil prices just after the CIA reportedly encouraged Kuwait to take advantage of Iraq's economic problems to pressure it into resolving the border dispute.

• Saudi Arabia also had encouraged Iraq's threats of military action against Kuwait to cow the emirate into following the pricing guidelines of the Organization of Petroleum Exporting Countries (OPEC).

• Despite her long-delayed, disingenuous denials before a cursory Congress eight months later, U.S. Ambassador April Glaspie did little to dissuade Hussein from invading Kuwait during her July 25, 1990, meeting with the Iraqi leader.

• Other members of the Bush administration defended Iraq against a growing number of congressional critics almost until the day of its invasion of Kuwait, and headed off a study of alleged abuses of Iraqi citizens by the U.N. Human Rights Commission earlier in the year.

• The United States, by accident or by design, apparently sabotaged an Arab summit to resolve the dispute between Iraq and Kuwait, after which Hussein had assured intermediaries he would withdraw his occupying troops.

• Contrary to Bush's later justification for sending the first contingent of U.S. troops to the region, satellite photos and radio intercepts indicated Iraq showed no signs of invading Saudi Arabia.

• The bases used by U.S. troops in Saudi Arabia had been secretly built for American use during just such a crisis, with "off-the-books" Saudi funds.

• Bush deliberately overstated Iraq's nuclear-weapons capabilities after surveys showed raising the issue could positively affect public opinion.

• The international embargo against Iraq had been far more effective than the U.S. government led its citizens to believe.

• The Iraqi military machine the U.S.-led coalition felt compelled to dismantle was largely of the coalition's own careless creation and, as it turned out, exaggeration.

• Contrary to the perception created by military briefers, precision-guided bombs made up barely 7 percent of the U.S. tonnage dropped on Iraqi targets. Of the bombs dropped during the war, 70 percent missed their targets.

• Again contrary to the public's perception, Patriot missiles usually failed to intercept incoming Scud missile warheads. Usually what they were seen intercepting on America's TV screens were the Scuds' discarded fuel tanks.

• The postwar costs of keeping American forces in the Middle East and building weapons systems that were unlikely to be approved before the perceived success of high-tech weapons during the war will cost the United States far more than the war itself.

For these and many other reasons, the U.S.-led military operation called Desert Storm was actually a Desert Mirage. And, like most mirages, Desert Mirage will cause a large letdown if those it deceived ever come to see it for what it really was: the pursuit of power disguised as the pursuit of principle—at a cost of tens of thousands of innocent lives.

A War of Words

To carry out its campaign of manipulation and deception, the Bush administration launched a three-pronged attack.

First, the United Nations and coalition members were brought—or bought—into line.

Second, the news media were first misled, then intimidated, and finally co-opted.

Third, military officials magnificently stage-managed the war through briefings that featured gamelike videos and desensitizing descriptions of civilian casualties as "collateral damage," U.S. casualties as "KIAs," and killing as "attriting."

Although allied soldiers who had been captured were still POWs, captured Iraqis became EPWs, or Enemy Prisoners of War. And when military commanders spoke of NBCs, they were talking about nuclear, biological, and chemical weapons, not the television network. Americans "engaged" the enemy instead of attacking him, and tanks were "neutralized" instead of being blown up.

Even the aim of the war itself had changed: Rather than defeating the enemy, we learned, the aim was "assertive disarmament."

To achieve that goal, the allied forces used "discriminate deterrence," previously known as precision bombing.

Nice ways to describe nasty events. But such words didn't develop by accident. They came about by design.

"The goal of euphemisms used in the military is to conceal completely, to deliberately give the wrong idea about something," Tom Fahey, author of *The Joys of Jargon,* told the *Orlando Sentinel.*

Stephen Becker, an English instructor at the University of Central Florida in Orlando, told the same paper that military language obfuscates the truth by stripping words and phrases of all emotion.

"The point when you're killing people or dealing with unpleasant subjects generally is to make the subjects as abstract as possible," Becker said. That was why, he added, we heard about "human remains pouches" instead of "body bags," we were told our forces had "serviced the adversary" instead of "blown the enemy to bits," and we learned of sophisticated "intelligence assets" rather than "spy satellites."

Saddam Hussein's terminology, on the other hand, was much more blunt in his fiery speeches: "We have prepared ourselves for burning the bodies of the corrupt and evil invaders, and our revenge will be devastating and ruthless," he said. "We will not hesitate and we will seek to turn the ground war into a hellfire that will sear their scoundrels. Their cohorts will tumble into the great crater of death."

"Treachery" proved to be such a favorite Saddamism that one couldn't help but wish the man would buy a thesaurus: "The treacherous committed treachery," he bellowed. "The despicable Bush and his treasonous agent Fahd, and all those who supported them in committing crimes, shame, and aggression, committed the treachery. Those cowards who have perfected the acts of treachery, treason, and vileness, committed treachery after they departed from every path of virtue, goodness, and humanity. They have committed treachery and launched their ground offensive."

But Hussein was not beyond subtle symbolism as well. The Iraqi dictator frequently referred to milk in his speeches, and claimed that the allies had bombed an infant-milk factory. These references were lost on most Americans, but milk is a powerful symbol in Islam, and Hussein was milking it for all it was worth.

J. R. McLeod, an expert on political rhetoric at Ohio State University, noted that "milk is really central to Arab life. It is a symbol of fertility, wealth, and life. So the charge that the war is depriving people, especially children, of milk is an emotionally charged message to Iraqis."

Although Hussein's words fell on deaf ears in the West, they had a definite impact in the Arab world. In addition to his references to milk, Hussein's description of the war as a *jihad*, or "holy war," gained him sympathy among Muslims, McLeod said.

Iraq also institutionalized the practice of disinformation through its state radio station. After the war started, the former Radio Baghdad became known as "Mother of Battles Radio," reflecting Hussein's attempt to portray the war as a holy war between Muslims and infidels.

When Iraqi troops invaded the lightly defended Saudi Arabian coastal town of Khafji, Mother of Battles Radio told Iraq's citizens, "Our valiant forces crushed the armies of infidelity in a lightning attack." Actually, coalition forces destroyed dozens of Iraqi tanks and armored vehicles and killed hundreds of Iraqi troops while sustaining only light losses.

Mother of Battles Radio also informed Iraqis that their allies around the world had launched "crushing hits" on American and allied facilities, even making Bush "a hostage in his 'black house.' "

After some initial hesitation, Mother of Battles Radio began giving extensive coverage to the bombing of civilian facilities, while totally ignoring damage to military ones.

Reports on Iraqi triumphs were interspersed with patriotic songs, readings from the Koran, and slogans hailing Hussein as the hero of "the historic movement of the Arab and Islamic nation."

One popular song included the verse, "O Saddam, the sword of manhood, you'll be safe and victorious." In the end, he was neither.

At the same time, Iraq was reportedly busy planting phony stories to stir up Muslim opposition to the war. One told of thousands of Egyptian women being taken to the front to entertain coalition forces. Another accused U.S. forces of rounding up thousands of defenseless residents of the poor Islamic nation of Bangladesh and transporting them to the gulf to fight for the anti-Iraq coalition.

And while Iraqi officials allowed the broadcast around the world of ghastly images of the charred bodies of civilian victims killed in an allied air attack of a Baghdad bomb shelter, no cameras were allowed anywhere near occupied Kuwait. In fact, Hussein promised to personally "chop the legs off" of any foreign reporter found in the Kuwaiti war theater. So the outside world never had a chance to see Kuwaiti victims of torture, or evidence of the executions reported by Amnesty International.

Overall, though, Hussein proved to be a poor propagandist. His early attempt to play the role of cuddly uncle on television with the children of his "foreign guests" earned him only outrage in the West. He further inflamed passions by posting his "guests" at potential bombing targets. His later reversal of the policy and release of the hostages did little to assuage the damage.

His biggest blunder of all, however, was his parading of battered captive pilots on television.

Bush, on the other hand, proved to be a master propagandist who knew how to speak to his audience.

Though the British openly spoke of the war as a battle for world power and oil, Bush painted it instead as a noble battle for freedom against aggression.

"Americans do not like to fight for material resources," McLeod said in a paper presented at the University of Iowa in late March. "They like to believe they are fighting for principles and causes.

That's why Bush has stressed that we are fighting for the freedom of Kuwait and for a new world order."

Linda Robertson, a professor specializing in propaganda at Hobart and William Smith Colleges, told *USA Today* that Bush had painted Hussein with a typical propaganda brush to transform him into an evil, Hitler-like madman.

"It's a simple tale, frequently told in times of war," she said. "It obscures any immediate cause of war or any immediate history in that area."

In contrast, she noted, the United States successfully presented itself as all-just and pure of purpose in its attempt to dislodge Hussein from Kuwait.

"Propaganda was used to make Hussein appear much larger than life," Robertson said. "That's typical of war propaganda, and so is the view that war is our only alternative, that neither the embargo nor negotiations would work.

"Our government has to convince people that we're up against a dangerous person, absolutely evil, that our motives are pure and there's no choice but war. That's the nature of propaganda."

War Is Peace

The British writer George Orwell warned us of just such a "criminalization of language" through propaganda, euphemisms, and half-truths in an essay titled "Politics and the English Language."

"In our time, political speech and writing are largely the defense of the indefensible," he wrote. "Thus political language has to consist largely of euphemism, question-begging, and sheer cloudy vagueness. Defenseless villages are bombarded from the air, the inhabitants driven out into the countryside, the cattle machine-gunned, the huts set on fire with incendiary bullets: This is called *pacification*."

It may sound like Orwell was writing about the American "pa-cification" program during the Vietnam War, but he wasn't. Orwell wrote those words in 1946, twenty years before American "paci-fication" efforts almost extinguished the Southeast Asian nation.

Later, in his novel *1984,* Orwell created a totalitarian society in which posters preached that "War is Peace," "Ignorance is Strength," and "Freedom is Slavery."

Could such phrases become part of our lexicon as well? Judging from the enthusiastic response of a war-happy American public to such abuses of language in 1991, it is not beyond the realm of possibility. And neither is censorship.

In an article headlined, "The New War Cry: Stop the Press," Richard Morin of the *Washington Post* wrote: "In news about the Gulf War, most Americans are happily willing to let the military tell reporters who, what, (CENSORED), when, (CENSORED) and (CENSORED)."

Why? Because, Morin said,

America has become deeply smitten with its high-tech warriors in the gulf. Public trust in the armed forces, as measured in a recent *Washington Post* poll, has surged to record heights: More than eight out of 10 Americans said they have confidence in the military. Fewer than one out of four express similar trust in the press.

Although most journalists chafe over press restrictions imposed in this conflict, a majority of all Americans reveal few concerns about censorship of war news—except that maybe there should be more of it, according to a recent survey. . . . Nearly eight out of ten respondents—79 percent—said they believe that censorship of the war news reports is a good idea; just 16 percent disagreed.

It was no secret to insiders how this occurred. One such insider is William Darryl Henderson, a retired U.S. Army colonel and author of *The Hollow Army: How the U.S. Army is Oversold and Undermanned.*

In an article that appeared in the *Los Angeles Times* at the height of the pro-military euphoria, Henderson wrote:

> Eight years ago the U.S. Army began sending key officers to classes on ways of marketing commercial products. They brought this knowledge back and used it on Congress, the White House, the public. Now they are using it in their tightly controlled press briefings in Saudi Arabia and at the Pentagon to maintain public support for the Gulf War.

According to Henderson, the military establishment learned the importance of maintaining continuous public support for a conflict during the Vietnam War, and it designed a strategy for selling the military's view of war:

> Good news is heavily marketed. Bad news is buried; it doesn't sell well. Bad news is managed in three basic ways: by restricting access to it; by presenting it as an isolated incident to be expected in the fog of war; by allowing it to dribble out in a controlled seepage over a number of days or weeks in order to avoid one big story with major negative impact.
>
> Bad news can't always be restricted and controlled, especially if low-ranking soldiers become aware of it. They will almost always tell, especially if the press has access to their units. But current press pool rules in the gulf cut off the press and public from these soldiers.

Instead, especially in the crucial early days of the war, the military kept the press and the American people as a whole enthralled with briefings designed to show high-tech warfare in its best light, while tough questions were ducked like incoming shells.

Entertaining, gamelike videos showed "smart bombs" surgically striking their targets. Reporters were told that Iraq's elite Republican Guard had been "decimated." Allied air strikes were said to have been 80 percent successful; it took the Pentagon ten days to admit that this meant only that a plane had reached its target and dropped its bombs, not that the "serviced asset" had been hit.

"There was no bad news," Henderson noted. "U.S. public reaction was as expected. Support for the war rose almost overnight from 47 to 80 percent."

Truth Drowns In Pool

The Pentagon's clever marketing strategy went far beyond the slick briefings and deliberate deception, however.

Reporters and photographers were barred from Dover Air Force Base, where the remains of dead servicemen and servicewomen arrived.

Battlefield photographs of American casualties were virtually nonexistent. Photos of dead Iraqis were also tightly controlled by the U.S. military—so much so that a photographer who tried to take one without permission was clubbed with a rifle by a soldier. Reporters were denied access to prisoner-of-war camps, B-52 pilots, AWACS planes, battleships, hospitals, and even chaplains—who had to be called "morale officers" in deference to their Muslim "hosts." There also were no estimates of enemy casualties.

As for the press pool system, it worked beautifully—for the Pentagon.

The one-hundred-plus pool reporters were chosen from among the 1,500 covering the war (about 2,000 covered the Super Bowl) on the basis of how long their news organizations had been in

Saudi Arabia. They were divided into groups and assigned to different military units, whose commanders decided where they could go and provided their transportation. That left reporters no freedom to pursue stories they considered important, which is why they began making unauthorized trips on their own.

"In effect," *New York Times* reporter Malcolm W. Browne wrote, "each pool member is an unpaid employee of the Department of Defense, on whose behalf he or she prepares the news of the war for the outer world."

As an example, Browne cited the experience he and Frank Bruni of the *Detroit Free Press* had on their first pool mission covering a briefing at the operations center for the radar-evading F-117A Stealth aircraft in Saudi Arabia.

After interviewing returning pilots and watching videos of the deadly accurate bombs they had dropped, the two wrote what they considered positive stories.

The censors didn't see it that way, however. They changed Bruni's description of the pilots from "giddy" to "proud." In Browne's story, "fighter-bomber" was changed to "fighter"—because, he suspected, the Air Force was waging a campaign to save the costly B-2 Stealth-bomber project, and any description of the F-117A as a "bomber" might be used by critics to argue that a second Stealth bomber wasn't necessary.

"To make newspaper deadlines, Bruni and I agree to the changes, on the condition that our copy is dispatched hastily, via fax machine, to pool headquarters in Dhahran," Browne wrote in the March 3 issue of the *New York Times Magazine*. "This proves to be a forlorn hope. We learn the following day that our stories have been sent instead to officials at the Tonopah Test Range in Nevada—the home base of the Stealth fighters—where everything we wrote has been deemed a breach of security." He continued:

More than 24 hours after they were written our stories are finally cleared, but of course, the war has already moved on and our perishable dispatches are hopelessly stale.

Next, we learn something new and vitally important: Our Stealth-pilot friends have smashed Iraq's laboratories and plants involved in developing nuclear weapons. . . . We ask the Stealth commander for permission to report the happy tidings, but he turns us down on the grounds that new attacks on the nuclear facilities might be needed and nothing should be reported until the job is completed.

We of course agree, but the following day Agence France-Presse, the French news agency, scoops us on the story by getting details of the raid from the staff of a U.S. senator. And the day after that Gen. H. Norman Schwarzkopf announces the raid himself.

Browne's experience was typical of what reporters faced. Unlike during every other major American conflict since World War II, correspondents weren't permitted on the battlefield without a controlling "military escort," some of whom tried to tell reporters what questions they could ask, and soldiers what answers they could give. Many of these "escorts" were often openly hostile to reporters, as were many officers.

"I've covered wars for twenty-five years and the first time I'm held prisoner is by my own military," Mort Rosenblum, a veteran Associated Press reporter was quoted as saying later.

Rosenblum told the *Los Angeles Times* that he and AP photographer Tannen Maury had gone north from Dhahran looking for a certain Army division. When they got to the division's headquarters, they stopped at a tent occupied by MPs.

"A guy came by who looked like an officer and I stopped him and asked to see the PAO [public affairs officer]," Rosenblum said. "He said, 'Not only will you see the PAO. You'll wait right here for him.' "

Rosenblum and Maury were placed under guard, and were told that if they tried to leave the MPs, machine-gun-equipped vehicles would been sent after them. They were finally released three hours later.

Journalists with the *New York Times,* the *Washington Post,* Cox Newspapers, and several other organizations were detained under similar circumstances. One of them, freelance photographer Wesley D. Bocxe, who was on assignment for *Time* magazine, was detained for thirty-six hours by the Alabama National Guard after he had stopped to take photos of a convoy of tanks miles south of the Kuwaiti border.

"I was spread-eagled across a Humvee [military vehicle] and searched and blindfolded," Bocxe told the *Los Angeles Times.* He said the MPs also accused him of faking his press credentials, and questioned him about spying for Iraq.

Bocxe was finally sent to the Joint Information Bureau, where he had little choice but to sign a copy of the ground rules, which stated that journalists could not travel without an escort or reveal sensitive information on troop locations or movements. Bocxe had previously refused to agree to the rules, but this time felt he had no choice.

But because Bocxe was represented by a French press agency that wasn't a member of the press pool, he was essentially sidelined from action.

In another incident, *New York Times* reporter Chris Hedges had just finished interviewing shopkeepers in Saudi Arabia when he was picked up by a U.S. military official, detained for almost three hours, and sent back to his hotel in Dhahran without his press credentials because he didn't have a military escort.

Stanley Cloud, *Time's* Washington bureau chief, told the *Washington Post* that asking questions about the pool system was "like asking whether a smoothly functioning dictatorship is working well."

"This is an intolerable effort by the government to manage

and control the press," he said. "We have ourselves to blame every bit as much as the Pentagon. We never should have agreed to this system in the first place."

Of course, the news media didn't have a whole lot of choice. The system was developed by the Pentagon in 1984 in the wake of a journalistic uproar after reporters had been completely excluded from the American invasion of Grenada.

The debate over access had begun in Vietnam, where journalists, bound only by a rule not to reveal sensitive military information, traveled wherever they could. In more than a decade, only a few reporters lost their credentials for inadvertently disclosing strategic information.

As a result, however, correspondents in the jungle began reporting that the war wasn't going as well as the officers in Saigon were claiming. Because public opinion began turning against the war at the same time, a belief evolved among the conflict's supporters that the media, not the military, lost the Vietnam War.

And journalists paid the price for that belief in the Persian Gulf War, even though a 1989 study by none other than the U.S. Army Center of Military History concluded that it was rising casualties and the lack of a winning strategy—and not news coverage —that had turned the public against the protracted conflict. In fact, the study went on to say that, despite some flaws, "the press reports were still often more accurate than the public statements of the administration in portraying the situation in Vietnam."

But that didn't stop the Pentagon from clamping down on the press in the Persian Gulf. In an attempt to have the restrictions removed, several publications, including the *Nation,* the *Village Voice,* and *Harper's,* and reporters like Sydney Schanberg of *Killing Fields* fame, sued the Pentagon in federal court.

The inadequacy of the pool system became increasingly apparent in the first ground battle of the Gulf War. During the thirty-six-hour-long ground battle at Khafji from January 29 to January

31, a press pool assigned to the U.S. Marines was kept far from the fighting, and pool members had no choice but to rely on information provided by officers from field headquarters, who played down the Marines' role, which had been considerable, and said the Iraqis were being beaten back with relative ease.

Reporters and photographers who made it into Khafji on their own or as part of a Saudi pool discovered a decidedly different scene of intense fighting in which Marine artillery units proved to be making the difference. But when U.S. public affairs officers arrived, they kicked the nonpool reporters out of town.

The pool reporters were then able to provide graphic stories about allied action, but they had to rely on the Saudi pool's reports on the surprising effectiveness with which Iraqi troops fought.

So when the shooting stopped, the shouting began. Journalists complained strongly that this was just the latest in a plethora of problems caused by a system that kept troops from speaking candidly and kept reporters from seeing things for themselves.

Tony Clifton of *Newsweek,* who had reported every major war since the 1960s, said he even had spent weeks trying unsuccessfully to contact an Air Force chaplain he had known for years who was based less than a mile from the press center, because rules didn't permit "unilateral" coverage outside the pools.

"In twenty years, the only nation I've found to be more restrictive—and not much more restrictive—was Iraq," he said. "I certainly saw more action with the Iraqis [against Iran] than now with the Americans," he told the Associated Press.

Greg English, an AP photographer who was not in a pool, agreed. "The last time I had so much trouble taking pictures was in South Africa," he said.

Most reporters quoted by AP in a story about the issue said the pool system was too restrictive and selective about what could be covered. They also complained about logistics problems, delays, and squelched details that distorted reality.

In one pool story, for example, a naval officer's reference to captured Iraqis was changed by an "escort" to refer to them as "rescued."

Leon Daniel, chief correspondent of United Press International, who has been covering wars since he was assigned to Vietnam in 1966, blamed reporters and editors for accepting the system, and said it was having an adverse effect on their independence.

"Segments of the press have already surrendered to the military minders," he told AP as the controversy brewed. "What you have is what the shrinks call the Stockholm syndrome [a tendency of hostages to eventually view their captors as allies]. The Pentagon uses the press as another weapon in its arsenal."

Broadcast reporters were equally outraged. "We are barred from even the most basic access," said CNN's Christiane Amanpour. "We are not allowed to report news. If we happened to stumble across news, we can't use it because it has to be cleared."

When fighter-bomber pilots returned after the air war started, she told AP, they were kept from the press for fourteen hours. Then the pilots were coached so much by public affairs officers before they went on camera that were uncertain about what to say.

Forrest Sawyer of ABC News, one of the first reporters into Kuwait City, said the pool system and restrictions in the Persian Gulf were "a travesty."

"The best and only real reporting I did was outside the pool system," Sawyer said in an interview with the *New York Daily News.* "None of us liked it. Reporting is about using your own initiative and going out and learning something of value to your public while staying within bounds of protecting operational security.

"The pool system devised by the Department of Defense is some strange, distorted form of public relations. The system is devised to control, edit, and limit the access of reporters from information. . . . [A] great deal of history was lost because of the pool process."

In fact, *Newsweek* reported in its first issue after the war that, "except for some archival footage shot by the military, historians will have no record of most of the actual fighting. As for the soldiers themselves, most of their heroic acts will go unwitnessed."

NBC correspondent Arthur Kent told AP that "the pools are effectively a branch of the U.S. military."

News Gets Grounded

Unfortunately, whether by accident or design, the military proved that it was a lot less efficient at processing news stories than it was at routing the Iraqis when the ground war was finally launched.

While reporters battled to interview troops, their stories often were bottled up at corps headquarters for so long that they had become irrelevant by the time they were released.

"It just didn't work," UPI's Leon Daniels told AP later. "My problem is with the whole concept of a miltary-run pool. Whoever said the Army is good at moving copy?"

In a few cases, elite units eagerly sought publicity to make themselves look good to the brass—and fund-granting congressmen back home. Some even offered helicopters and combat radios to get word back from the front. But there were far more cases in which the news simply died in the desert.

According to an AP report, the VII Corps' massive flanking movement through Iraq and into Kuwait never got the attention it deserved because reporters waited in vain for couriers to relay their stories.

Some reporters had to wait as long as a week to get out their stories on the troops' bravery and efficiency.

"We gave up lots of freedom to join the pool with the understanding that we would be allowed to do our work, but we were not allowed to do our work," Phil Shenon of the *New York Times* told AP.

The Associated Press said it had plenty of problems of its own, too. Three AP reporters covering VII Corps units had stories delayed several days. One said he spent ten days with a unit without being able to file a single story. Word got out only when a commander made a helicopter available to fly him back to a telephone center in Saudi Arabia.

The danger for nonpool reporters was underscored when CBS reporter Bob Simon and his crew, traveling on their own, disappeared near the Iraqi border and were held in Baghdad until the end of the war.

But Sydney Schanberg told the *Washington Post* that providing reporters with military vehicles and escorts is "the worst possible thing for a civilian's health. It's like putting a bulls-eye on you."

Associated Press photographer Bob Jordan discovered that the hard way when he was sent out with an escort officer in a rattletrap First Infantry Division car with a hot-wired ignition and flashlights strapped to the hood as headlights.

The officer had no radio. He had no map. He had no working compass. As a result, they spent two days wandering the desert, during which time they almost ran out of water. At one point, the car just missed a field of live ordnance. Then it blundered into an Iraqi bunker complex, where armed enemy troops watched as the two Americans changed a flat tire.

Many reporters said the needless delays proved that a pool system run by the military was bound to be a failure.

"The military needs to get out of the journalism business and we need to get back into it," said UPI's Daniels.

The manipulation of the news media reached a climax during allied commander Gen. H. Norman Schwarzkopf's virtuoso performance at a briefing after the liberation of Kuwait City on February 27.

Schwarzkopf, whom NBC's Fred Francis had described as "a cross between Willard Scott, Jonathan Winters, and Attila the Hun," authoritatively went through maps and charts as he analyzed the rout of Hussein's sorry excuse for an army. The avuncular general sounded like a coach who had just won the Super Bowl, with the exception that he expressed open disgust rather than respect for his defeated opponent.

Asked for his assessment of the military skills of Hussein, Schwarzkopf said sarcastically, "He is neither a strategist, nor is he a general, nor is he a soldier. Other that that, he's a great military man."

So why had President Bush profiled him as the second coming of Adolf Hitler?

Reporters didn't ask. Nor did they ask many other questions of merit as they put up only light resistance to the general's verbal barrage. In fact, Schwarzkopf refused to answer the only two tough questions he was asked—one about the Iraqi casualties, the other about why the allies continued to bomb Baghdad. But that was par for the course. Reporters had become resigned to the fact that military briefers didn't answer important questions.

"I'll get back to you on that," they would say time after time. But, of course, they rarely did.

At one point in a briefing about the controversial destruction of what the Pentagon said was a military shelter that contained hundreds of civilians, increasingly tough questions prompted a frustrated Army Lt. Gen. Thomas Kelly to tell reporters: "Everything that we're seeing relative to this facility is coming out of a controlled press in Baghdad. So we don't know what all the facts are. We don't have a free press there asking hard questions like you all do here."

But the reporters had a good reason to be skeptical: The Pentagon and White House have a long history of statements that turned out to be misleading or untrue.

During the Korean War, for example, Gen. Douglas A. Mac-Arthur issued misleading reports on the Chinese rout of U.S. troops at Chosin Reservoir.

During Vietnam, government accounts of the Tonkin Gulf incident of 1964, which provoked a congressional resolution President Lyndon B. Johnson later used to justify escalation of the war, turned out to have been inaccurate in several respects. Later, reporters were told repeatedly that the war was being won, when just the opposite was true. It was also during the Vietnam War that Assistant Secretary of Defense Arthur Sylvester said it was "the government's inherent right to lie, if necessary."

That appeared to be the case in 1983, when White House spokesman Larry Speakes told the press that reports that the United States was sending troops into Grenada were "preposterous," only to announce the invasion the next morning. After leaving his post at the White House, Speakes admitted in his memoirs that he had made up quotations he had attributed to President Reagan.

Media distrust became even greater when the *Washington Post* revealed in 1987 the existence of a "disinformation" campaign against Libya during which the press had been given incorrect information. A month later, Attorney General Edwin Meese III revealed that the Reagan administration, which had repeatedly claimed it had no secret dealings with Iran, had been selling arms to the Iranian government and sending the money to the contra rebels in Nicaragua.

Finally, after the *USS Vincennes* shot down an unarmed commercial Iranian airliner over the Persian Gulf in July 1988, killing almost three hundred people, Adm. William J. Crowe Jr. said the airliner had been flying outside designated commercial air corridors, descending toward the *Vincennes,* and had failed to identify itself on commercial radio channels—all of which turned out to be dubious or untrue.

While many Americans were so incensed by media whining

about Pentagon censorship during the war that they began to openly call reporters "traitors," Schwarzkopf showed that they had actually been dupes.

At his post-victory press conference, Schwarzkopf told the press that it had been a convenient conduit for disinformation. He cited, in particular, how extensive coverage of the mock amphibious attacks on Kuwait in the fall of 1990 had helped to deceive the Iraqis.

Schwarzkopf said he had wanted Hussein to believe the allies would make major forays onto the beaches in eastern Kuwait so he would keep his troops concentrated there while the allies moved west and north in a flanking action.

Alluding to the generous coverage of the mock attacks, Schwarzkopf thanked the journalists for their support. He just laughed when asked if he would reveal other ways in which the media had been used.

But even without his revelations, there was plenty of evidence of additional media manipulation.

In one early case, *Newsweek* reported in its January 28 issue, Schwarzkopf "resorted to outright deception" to make Hussein think the United States had more troops at the base in Dhahran than it actually did. "The Pentagon orchestrated a stream of public announcements of units deployed in the gulf; the statements left out the fact that only elements of these units had actually been sent," *Newsweek* reported. "Saddam had no satellites or spy planes to watch the buildup; he got much of his intelligence from CNN.

"So Schwarzkopf made sure television crews were out each day shooting the giant C-5 Galaxy transports that landed every few minutes in Dhahran."

Ironically, the most potentially damaging security leaks were those allowed by military censors. After the cease-fire, one high-ranking military official instrumental in trying to manage the press at the Pentagon was quoted as saying: "We are guilty of contributing to the release of some very important information that could have been very helpful to the enemy."

One such security breach was a censor's approval of a January 23 pool report that mentioned near the end that allied engineers were working in the western Saudi Arabian town of Rahfa.

By reading later pool reports and talking to sources, Pentagon correspondents for CBS, NBC, the *Washington Post, U.S. News & World Report,* and a few other organizations figured out the secret plan to rush north into Iraq to Nasiriyah, where the allies cut off the Iraqi retreat. But the reporters kept the information to themselves to protect the very national security the public was so convinced reporters would damage if not censored.

The press knowingly helped the Pentagon in other ways, too. A senior military official told members of the first press pool to arrive in Saudi Arabia in August that "we are going to be vulnerable for a while, and you would do a great deal of danger if you focus on that weakness." The reporters agreed to ignore the vulnerability.

Later, false reports of Air Force landings in Kuwait and Iraq were planted by the military with Saudi and Kuwaiti news agencies, and, in an attempt to encourage defections, the CIA planted a false story that sixty Iraqi tank crews had defected.

In Washington, meanwhile, the Bush administration did its best to use the same "spin control" and "message of the day" propaganda techniques it had used so successfully during the 1988 presidential campaign.

In an example of the latter, Secretary of Defense Dick Cheney referred to Iraqi Scud missiles during an interview as "weapons of terror." As the interview progressed, Cheney began to refer to *all* Iraqi missiles as "weapons of terror." Later, President Bush suddenly began using the same term in what was obviously a carefully crafted effort to plant the term in the public consciousness. And it worked. Soon it seemed that everyone was referring to

Scu ᵈˢ as "weapons of terror"—as if the missiles and smart bombs hitting Baghdad weren't "weapons of terror" as well.

Accusations of censorship and media manipulation reached a climax on February 20, when the British-based censorship watchdog group Article 19—whose name derives from the U.N. Universal Declaration of Human Rights section that upholds freedom of the press—accused allied military forces of using reporting restrictions to "filter and mold" news of the war.

An Article 19 report, "Stop the Press: The Gulf War and Censorship," gave almost a hundred examples of how U.S., British, French, and other allied forces were tailoring information to gain their own objectives.

"Coalition forces have imposed sanctions such as confiscation of equipment of journalists who do not abide by the ground rules, and have even recommended deportation," the report charged.

It also complained that military censors had been taking up to three days to clear news reports, giving the military the power "to shape news."

Article 19 said the United States had taken "unprecedented steps" to control the flow of information, including giving Saudi Arabian authorities the names of American journalists who tried to report independent of military censors, after which the Saudis threatened to expel them.

In some cases, the report said, U.S. censors had demanded deletion of nonsensitive quotes and information from the field to give a more favorable impression. For example, an article from the aircraft carrier *USS Kennedy* was suppressed because it described pilots watching pornographic films before take-off. In other reports, Article 19 charged, pilots' quotations containing profanity were needlessly deleted.

The report also claimed that Saudi Arabia had banned many foreign newspapers; others were strongly censored, with reports mentioning civilian casualties being cut. In addition, Turkey blacked out CNN reports that U.S. aircraft used Turkish air bases to launch attacks on Iraq.

In Washington, on the same day the Article 19 report was released, three correspondents recently back from the war zone told the Senate Governmental Operations Committee that the Pentagon system of limiting coverage to a handful of journalists had stifled accurate accounts of the war.

Malcolm W. Browne of the *New York Times,* Cragg Hines of the *Houston Chronicle,* and Frank Aukofer of the *Milwaukee Journal* said the pool system had been originally proposed as a temporary measure to get at least a few reporters to the field during the early hours of an engagement.

After that, reporters were supposed to be free to cover the war on their own, they said, but Pentagon procedures made such coverage almost impossible.

"Exclusive coverage by pools allows military commanders to veto coverage of their units or to arrange it to their self-promoting advantage," Hines said.

Browne, who won a Pulitzer Prize for his reporting from Vietnam for the Associated Press, said the only comparable censorship he had experienced was a news blackout imposed by Pakistan, the losing side, during its 1971 war with India.

Also weighing in was retired CBS anchorman Walter Cronkite.

"With an arrogance foreign to the democratic system, the U.S. military in Saudi Arabia is trampling on the American people's right to know," Cronkite warned. "It is doing a disservice not only to the home front but also to history and its own best interests."

Noting the public's apparent support of military censorship, Cronkite added:

After World War II most Germans protested that they did not
know what went on in the heinous Nazi concentration camps.
But this claim of ignorance did not absolve them of blame:

They had complacently permitted Hitler to do his dirty business in the dark. They raised little objection, most even applauded when he closed newspapers and clamped down on free speech. Certainly our leaders are not to be compared with Hitler, but today, because of onerous, unnecessary rules, Americans are not being permitted to see and hear the full story of what their military forces are doing in an action that will reverberate long into the nation's future.

Cronkite said the Pentagon's pool system was doing the public such a disservice that he would prefer that reporters be censored but free to range over the battle front. He said reporters should be put in uniform and permitted to go to wherever the action was, with their dispatches or television tape subject to review only for military secrets.

That was the method in use when he covered World War II as a young United Press correspondent, he said, and it worked to everyone's advantage.

"The fact that the military apparently feels there is something it must hide can only lead eventually to a breakdown in home-front confidence and the very echoes from Vietnam that the Pentagon fears most," Cronkite warned.

But the news media weren't without their internal critics. Journalists and journalism educators participating in a discussion of the military and the media at Boston University generally blamed the media, rather than the government, for what they called the military's overwhelming success in controlling information, according to a *Boston Globe* report.

Some said the press was badly prepared to cover the war despite months of indications that the conflict was coming, and blamed journalists for not fighting the restrictions imposed on them more strenuously before the war started.

"The control of information flowing to the public through

the press is the most complete that I know of," said William Kovach, curator of the Nieman Foundation at Harvard. "Maybe the German High Command in the runup to World War II had as much, but you have to go back that far."

John Hart, host of Christian Science Broadcasting's *World Monitor,* contended that reporters were neglecting what the public needed to know when they concentrated on questions of strategy. "What the public needs to know is not the intent but the consequence," Hart said. "There is a sense of unreality in the reporting so far, which has been given us by the military briefers."

H. Joachim Maitre, dean of Boston University's College of Communication, said the no-news news conferences held by the military were a farce, and that reporters were "completely in the hands of the government."

Kovach said correspondents reported all the early glowing military reports with such blind enthusiasm that "anyone reading a newspaper or watching television in the first two or three days of the war would conclude with good cause that the war could be over in about 26 minutes."

Hart added that "television had failed spectacularly" to supply the information the public needed to understand the many aspects of the conflict. Especially important, he said, was the need to broaden awareness of Arab history and religion.

"The military learned from Vietnam not to count bodies," he said. "The public learned from Vietnam not to blame soldiers. What we did not learn from Vietnam is that we need to know the people we are fighting against."

But the conservative syndicated columnist Georgie Anne Geyer viewed the media's performance quite differently.

"As the world can see at the euphoric end of the Gulf War, the much-feared 'class war' in the Arab world never occurred," she wrote, adding:

But a new and real class war did occur. It revealed itself day after day in the military briefing rooms in Dhahran and on the television screens of the nation. There many of the new (largely) young reporters of the upper-class American suburbs confronted the (largely) young working-class soldiers of the new volunteer army.

In case you still wonder who won that war, consider that 80 percent of Americans polled say they approve of military restrictions on the press and 62 percent said we should bomb the Baghdad hotel where journalists were staying—after only one warning!

Ladies and gentlemen of our press and media, editors and publishers, my dear friends and dedicated colleagues: We are in trouble! Despite the great courage of so many journalists and correspondents, despite the dogged reporting, despite the fact that the military was partly to blame with its unrealistic new regulations, we lost this one.

Geyer blamed the media's defeat on their "adversarial antagonism toward just about everybody."

From Watchdog to Puppydog

But that "adversarial antagonism" certainly wasn't in evidence when the ground war began on February 25. The networks in particular, one critic noted, looked more like puppydogs than watchdogs as they accepted almost everything that came out of the Pentagon and White House, including the rationale for a needless news blackout. Even worse, they didn't discuss the discomfiting questions about whether the ground attack was even necessary or justified.

The jingoistic coverage at that point was typified by this war update by CBS anchor Dan Rather during the halftime of a college basketball game: "The allied fast-break offense is running, gunning, and going good."

But Rather wasn't alone. During a halftime report on NBC, Tom Brokaw boasted that early reports indicated "this is a blowout for the allied forces."

Andrew Tyndall, a former NBC research consultant who publishes a newsletter analyzing network news, told the *Philadelphia Inquirer,* "The networks have treated this war as a technical military exercise," which is just how the White House wanted it.

Jeff Cohen, director of Fairness & Accuracy in Reporting, a liberal media watchdog, agreed. "Some of the stuff on the news has been beyond belief: 'We' and 'our troops.' It's symbolic of the whole problem," he said.

Cohen said that the networks "filled air time with one of the most one-sided lists of experts I've ever seen. . . . Their idea of 'balance' is to bring in Democrats who support the war, like Stephen Solarz, Les Aspin, and Lee Hamilton."

After monitoring ABC, NBC, and CBS nightly news shows during the five months before the war, FAIR also concluded that only 1 percent of the gulf coverage dealt with grass-roots opposition to the troop buildup. Large anti-war demonstrations that took place shortly after the war started received scant attention.

Alex Molnar, the father of a Marine in Saudi Arabia whose poignant open letter appearing in the *New York Times* criticized President Bush's policies and led to the founding of the Military Families Support Network, couldn't even get the group's paid thirty-second commercial on the air. CNN and the three network-owned television stations in Washington all rejected the spot because it was deemed to be unbalanced.

According to the *San Jose Mercury News,* the Los Angeles chapter of Physicians for Social Responsibility had the same problem when it tried to place an anti-war commercial on CNN and on the New York and Los Angeles affiliates of ABC and CBS.

At the same time, retired officers were dominating the airwaves as supposedly objective military analysts. CNN even sank so low as to use retired Maj. Gen. Richard V. Secord, who in 1990 pleaded guilty to perjury in connection with the Iran-contra scandal. The news network's endless parade of retired generals, each drawing lines on maps and satellite photos of Kuwait with Telestrators like those used by ex-coaches to analyze sports contests, finally prompted columnist Richard Reeves to suggest that CNN call itself PNN—the Pentagon News Network.

Skepticism surfaced only rarely during the war's final days. Bob Faw of CBS stood pretty much alone, for example, when he reported from the United Nations that Bush's order to start the ground war while the Security Council was still trying to negotiate a peace agreement was "somewhat embarrassing, if you will, for the U.N., leaving this institution sitting on the sidelines and suggesting that when push comes to shove, this place is little more than what its critics always said it was—a glorified debating society and not a force to be reckoned with."

Implicit in his comment was that the start of the ground war showed Bush relied on the world body only when it was convenient to do so. Of course, that shouldn't come as a big surprise. Only a little more than a year before, Bush had totally ignored a General Assembly condemnation of the invasion of Panama he had ordered.

For the most part, though, the networks paraded a veritable *Who's Who* of the Bush administration and congressional leaders to defend the massive military effort. Perhaps the worst flag-waving came from correspondent Jack Smith in a Sunday morning cheerleading exercise on ABC's *This Week With David Brinkley,* in which he defended every aspect of Bush's policy, including the "unstated but crucial objective" of humbling Hussein.

Smith supported his biased conclusion with sound bites from the ubiquitous, supposedly omniscient Henry Kissinger and two other GOP gadflies, Geoffrey Kemp and David Gergen.

This came in complete contrast to correspondents' comments a few days earlier about "the Pentagon's worst fear," something that might place Bush "in a bad position," a potential "tragedy" that apparently had to be avoided at all costs.

This dragon to be slain was a last-minute Soviet-brokered peace plan. The fact that it would be a peace with victory and would force Iraq's withdrawal from Kuwait didn't seem to matter. It was a peace Bush didn't want, and at this point Bush was deemed to have earned the right to have anything he wanted and to reject out of hand anything he didn't.

To be fair, the obsequious deference showed to the president, by network reporters in particular, at the end of the war came only after an intensive effort to intimidate, manipulate, undermine, and question the patriotism of any reporter who didn't report what Bush deemed appropriate.

Whenever a reporter didn't fit the mold, the administration's verbal hit men began to play hardball.

Their top target was Peter Arnett of CNN, who was attacked for reports on allied bomb damage in Baghdad's residential areas, even though Arnett and CNN had made it clear that his Iraqi escorts had shown him only what they wanted him to see.

As Arnett's reports began to sink in with the public, he was accused of being an Iraqi "sympathizer" by Sen. Alan Simpson, a Republican from Wyoming who only a year before had been in Baghdad himself, advising our then-ally Saddam Hussein that his problem was the American press—not the U.S. government.

Arnett, Simpson told a group of reporters, "was active in the Vietnam War and he won a Pulitzer Prize largely because of his anti-government material. And he was married to a Vietnamese whose brother was active in the Viet Cong. I called that 'sympathizer' in my early days in the Second World War."

White House officials also ripped into Arnett when he reported that Iraq had accused the United States of bombing that nation's only infant-formula plant.

White House spokesman Marlin Fitzwater insisted that the plant was a biological weapons facility.

But Michel Wery, director of Pierre Guerin, the French company that built the plant, told the Paris newspaper *Liberation* that the plant actually had produced infant formula and baby food. The *Washington Post* quoted Wery as saying that the plant had been built as an infant-formula factory in a Baghdad industrial area during the 1970s, and that it would be impossible to convert its equipment to manufacture biological weapons.

Two New Zealand dairy engineers who helped Iraq set up a cheese factory near the site also were quoted as saying they doubted the U.S. account of how the plant was being used. The technicians, who said they visited the plant as recently as the previous May, told the newspaper they had seen machinery "actually canning milk powder."

When asked about the reports, three administration officials who asked not to be identified gave different accounts of the plant's operations.

A White House official said the plant had been turned into a biological warfare facility last fall, an official of another agency said it was a backup germ warfare plant, and an official at a third agency said it was not a full-scale germ warfare plant but only made products that would be useful in germ warfare production.

When he was finally forced to leave Baghdad on March 8, Arnett expressed little surprise about being labeled an Iraqi sympathizer. "It comes with the territory of being a reporter . . . kill the messenger," he told CNN talk-show host Larry King in a live interview from Amman, Jordan.

Arnett stressed that his censored coverage from Baghdad "was a tiny segment of what CNN produced on a 24-hour basis."

"I was contributing such a little sliver that I felt that if there was a little unbalance there it would be well compensated by the Pentagon, Saudi, British briefings, and other information that came over the pike," he said.

Arnett added that he had no reason to doubt that the bombed Baghdad building Iraqi authorities told him was a baby milk factory was just that.

"It still looks like a baby milk factory to me," he told King. "I would concede that some of the other so-called civilian targets I saw may not have been entirely what they were said to be. But the baby milk factory—I went through it twice [and] every other journalist who went to Baghdad went through it—I was up to my knees in baby milk, infant formula, and I still don't see how it could have been a very highly specialized plant for chemical weapons, biological testing."

Concerning the bomb shelter hit by allied smart bombs, Arnett said, "To this day I still haven't seen any clear evidence, or any evidence, that it was used for military purposes."

Arnett also denied Simpson's allegation that he had had a brother-in-law who was a member of the Viet Cong. To the contrary, he said, one of his ex-wife's brothers had been killed by the Viet Cong, and the other was an officer in the Republic of Vietnam's U.S.-backed army.

Despite the apparent prevarication, though, Simpson's scurrilous "sympathizer" label for Arnett stuck with some Americans. In front of CNN headquarters in Atlanta, people protested against the once-highly respected reporter, who had probably seen more combat than any general in a thirty-year career during which he had covered sixteen wars and insurrections prior to his Baghdad assignment. He even became the butt of late-night talk-show jokes. Jay Leno, for example, remarked that "CNN has produced its first feature-length film about the Gulf War, starring Peter Arnett. It's called *Sleeping With the Enemy.*"

The Republican National Committee and other conservative

organizations exploited such sentiments to the hilt. For its part, the RNC sent a half-million party contributors preprinted anti-press letters to the editor. Recipients were asked to sign the letters, which urged support for the troops and denounced the media for giving "so much attention to the small number of anti-war protesters," and to use the accompanying preaddressed envelopes to mail the letters to their local papers.

Although an RNC spokesman insisted the effort was "not press-bashing," it hardly seems coincidental that the appeal was signed by none other than the apparently press-bashing Senator Simpson.

At the same time, Accuracy in Media, a conservative watchdog group, launched a massive letter-writing campaign to get Arnett out of Baghdad. AIM mailed a hundred-thousand postcards to supporters, urging them to demand Arnett's removal.

"CNN is keeping Peter Arnett in Baghdad to broadcast propaganda for Saddam Hussein, who wants to (1) undermine our morale and (2) disrupt the coalition by inflaming the Arabs against us," the postcards said. "If Arnett were not helping him, Saddam would pull the plug on him instantly. CNN should pull the plug. . . . Arnett's reporting from Vietnam helped the communists just as his reports from Baghdad help Saddam."

AIM founder Reed Irvine said the campaign was necessary because Arnett's broadcasts were "a betrayal of the troops." It was ludicrous, he said, for reporters to cling to the idea of a free press while soldiers were risking their lives.

Truth Slowly Seeps Out

Despite the multitude of efforts to discredit the news media, though, it was the government's credibility that began to suffer when the "record" oil spill it had blamed on Hussein turned out to be smaller than claimed and not solely the work of Iraq.

Officials originally called it the biggest spill ever, anywhere from twelve to forty-two times as large as the controversial *Exxon Valdez* disaster.

But later, independent experts said the "spill" was actually a series of spills, and that the total area covered was much smaller than officials had said. What's more, Saudi experts finally admitted that as much as 30 percent of the mess had resulted from allied bombing.

The propaganda value of the original charges was immense, however. President Bush quickly branded Hussein an "ecoterrorist," and said the spill didn't "measure up to any military doctrine of any kind. It's kind of sick." That it may have been. But using environmental destruction as a tool of war has a long and effective history going back to 146 B.C., when the Romans laid waste to the Carthaginians' fields by spreading salt on them and continuing right through the United States' use of poisonous herbicides in Vietnam.

In fact, the administration had been concerned enough about Hussein's threats to use Kuwait's oil as a weapon if attacked that in the fall of 1990 it commissioned top-secret studies on "environmental impacts of fires/oil spills in the Middle East," according to an article by John Horgan in the May 1991 issue of *Scientific American*. The studies concluded that the smoke's impact on U.S. weapons would be minimal. Estimates on damage to the world climate and environment varied. The local impact, on the other hand, was properly predicted to be potentially immense.

Raymond Henry, an American firefighting expert, was quoted as saying that Kuwait had suffered an environmental "catastrophe," and that was almost an understatement. Temperatures under the thick clouds of smoke were far below normal during the day, hospitals were packed with patients suffering from respiratory problems, and "black rain" damaged crops and drinking water. The long-term effects are expected to be considerable.

As for the rest of the world, some predicted an acceleration in global warming because of as much as a 5 percent increase in carbon dioxide emissions, while others forecast something similar to a "nuclear winter" as a byproduct of the thirty million tons of smoke the burning wells were expected to produce in a year.

Even one of the more optimistic experts quoted by Horgan forecast dire consequences. "We have never seen a pollution event of this scale," said Richard Small of the Pacific-Sierra Research Corp. Its impact, he added, might be felt as much as 1,000 kilometers from Kuwait.

But the history of using environmental destruction as a weapon and the fact that the United States knew of the risk it was taking at the start of the war was lost in Bush's "ecoterrorist" rhetoric. That was just one example of how Bush proved to be a perfect propagandist throughout the Persian Gulf crisis as he slowly built public support for a war that a large majority originally opposed.

After almost ten years of trying to make Hussein look as good as possible, Bush and his fellow Republicans suddenly turned him into the Willie Horton of world politics by portraying him as a demon-like dictator whose insane ambitions were a threat to the entire world order.

In addition to all those public insults, Bush reportedly hurled private ones every time he mispronounced the Iraqi leader's name. According to the April issue of *Washingtonian* magazine, the CIA suggested that Bush pronounce it "SAD-dam" because with that emphasis the word's meaning was changed from "one who confronts" to "a little boy who cleans out the shoes of old men."

One of the president's most effective public weapons was an Amnesty International report issued in December on Iraqi atrocities in Kuwait.

The president began telling almost anyone who would listen that the Nobel Peace Prize–winning group's gruesome document should be "compulsory reading."

In early January, Bush used Amnesty's report as the basis of a column sent to the nation's college newspapers, in which he wrote:

> There is much in the modern world that is subject to doubts or question—washed in shades of gray. But not the brutal aggression of Saddam Hussein against a peaceful, sovereign nation and its people. It's black and white. The facts are clear. The choice unambiguous.
>
> Right vs. wrong. The terror Saddam Hussein has imposed upon Kuwait violates every principle of human decency. Listen to what Amnesty International has documented: "Widespread abuses of human rights have been perpetrated by Iraqi forces . . . arbitrary arrest and detention without trial of thousands . . . widespread torture . . . imposition of the death penalty and extra-judicial execution of hundreds of unarmed civilians, including children."

With that effort to exploit the report, John G. Healey, executive director of Amnesty International USA, decided he had to speak out—although the press release he issued was largely ignored. In it he said he was "deeply distressed by the selective use" of the report and by Bush's "opportunistic manipulation of the international human-rights movement." He added:

> When taken at face value, President Bush's condemnation of torture and political killings by Iraqi authorities appears laudable. The matter becomes less "clear" and "unambiguous," however, in the light of two questions: Why did our president remain mute on the subject of the Iraqi government's patterns of severe human-rights abuses prior to August 1990? Why does he remain mute about abuses committed by other governments, our so-called coalition partners in the region?
>
> There was no presidential indignation . . . in 1989, when

Amnesty released its findings about the torture of Iraqi children. And just a few weeks before the invasion of Kuwait, the Bush administration refused to conclude that Iraq had engaged in a consistent pattern of gross human-rights violations.

If U.S. policies before last August "had reflected concern about the Iraqi government's human-rights record," Healey added, "our country might not be [at] war today."

He also noted that Bush's allies in Syria, Saudi Arabia, Turkey, and Egypt all routinely tortured and held without charges or trial thousands of political prisoners:

> President Bush's selective indignation over Iraq's abuses in Kuwait undermines the norms of "human decency" he touts in his letter to campus newspapers. All people in all countries are entitled to human-rights protection: International humanitarian standards rest upon this principle. The standards are unequivocally practical, because human-rights protection establishes a foundation for just, peaceful, stable order. Exploiting human rights to justify violent confrontation is itself indecent.

Unfortunately, things didn't get any better with our Persian Gulf allies after Healey made that accusation. On February 8, the group's international headquarters in London said both sides in the Persian Gulf War were allowing human rights to become a casualty of the conflict. It cited Britain's detention of Arabs, Iraqi treatment of prisoners of war, and actions by the governments of Saudi Arabia and Egypt. The organization restated its claim that a U.S. soldier from Michigan jailed after he refused to go to Saudi Arabia was a "prisoner of conscience."

And while the United States condemned Iraq's abuse of its Kurdish minority, it said nothing about a February 8 report by the Human Rights Association that Turkish forces had recently removed fifty thousand Kurds from three hundred villages and burned their homes. The group added that twenty-five hundred Kurds had been killed by Turkish troops in the past two years.

The United States also ignored Turkey's open flouting of a U.N. Security Council resolution demanding its withdrawal from Cyprus—part of which it has occupied since a 1974 invasion— just as it ignored a condemnation of its 1989 invasion of Panama and U.N. resolutions demanding Israel's withdrawal from the West Bank and Gaza Strip.

The world obviously is rife with inhumanity. The consistent condemnation of that inhumanity wherever and whenever it occurs would do more to stop it than the greatest inhumanity of them all—war. But President Bush apparently didn't see it that way.

As it turned out, there was also some question about the accuracy of the Amnesty report. Middle East Watch, an equally respected human-rights organization with more experience in the Persian Gulf, said that while atrocities had undoubtedly occurred after Iraq invaded Kuwait, they hadn't been nearly as numerous as Amnesty International had reported. And, in fact, an Amnesty International spokesperson later told the author that the organization was beginning to suspect it had been misled by several Kuwaiti doctors on whose information part of the report had been based.

Others have noted that much of the carnage that took place in Kuwait City apparently occurred only *after* the war had begun.

Amnesty's admission that it may have been partly deceived would seem to support Middle East Watch's suggestion that the respected organization had been too easily swayed by the aggressive war of words being waged by Kuwait's hired public-relations guns.

Kuwait Blitzes America

The size and scope of Kuwait's public-relations effort in the United States and the amount of money it was paying the huge—and expensive—New York's Hill & Knowlton Inc. and several other firms to wage its war of words was a closely guarded secret. But the truth about Hill & Knowlton's efforts finally surfaced when the firm, as required by law, filed records with the U.S. Justice Department's foreign agents registration office.

Those records showed that Hill & Knowlton had been paid $5.64 million for the period between August 20 and November 10 to promote the small-but-wealthy country's cause.

Frank Mankiewicz, a politically well-connected senior Hill & Knowlton executive, told a reporter that Kuwait's account was for "a big job on a big stage. . . . The assignment is to be effective."

To fulfill that objective, Hill & Knowlton's report showed, the firm had spent $2.7 million of the $5.64 million it had received, including $644,571 for video production and $140,412 for travel.

"It's a ridiculous sum of money no matter what you think of the cause," declared Representative James A. Hayes, a Louisiana Democrat. "When all of this is over, I think we should reassess the lines we have blurred on allowing other governments to have enormous influence on our political process."

The records showed that Citizens for a Free Kuwait, a group founded by thirteen Kuwaitis then living in the United States, hired Hill & Knowlton to "provide counsel on a national media program, strategic planning, and message development."

The Washington-based group got most of its money from the Kuwaiti government-in-exile in Saudi Arabia and London, where it was busy running its $100 billion foreign financial empire.

One of Hill & Knowlton's most successful efforts came when the firm coordinated the testimony of Kuwaiti refugees before the U.N. Security Council. Their headline-grabbing tales of rape and pillage by the Iraqi troops came just before a key U.N. vote authorizing the use of force against Iraq.

The PR blitz also included newspaper ads, lunches for journalists, public-opinion surveys, and a congressional hearing on Iraqi atrocities. Some other pro-war campaigns also had possible Kuwaiti links. The *New York Times* provided one such example when it reported that a former co-chairman of the Coalition for America at Risk, which ran a print and broadcast advertising campaign supporting Bush's military efforts, also happened to be a registered agent for the Kuwaiti Emergency Relief Fund.

But hiring others to do their dirty work—whether it be public relations, manual labor, domestic work, or fighting for their country—is a well-entrenched Kuwaiti custom.

According to one news report from Saudi Arabia, at least some Kuwaitis were less than proud of their fellow citizens' lack of pride and drive.

The story quoted a Kuwaiti army lieutenant as saying he couldn't help but feel shame at how easily and quickly Kuwait fell to Iraq.

Much of the army, other officers were quoted as saying, had been on vacation when the invasion came, even though the war drums in the Persian Gulf had been getting louder for two weeks prior to the invasion.

They even recited a joke about how little Kuwait's oil-rich people do for themselves: When a Kuwaiti was asked if sex is work or pleasure, they said, he replied, "It must be pleasure. If it was work, we'd hire a Pakistani to do it."

Or, when it comes to fighting, it soon seemed obvious, an American.

So as Americans and others were liberating Kuwait, Egyptians were looking forward to liberating themselves from the thousands of rich Kuwaitis who had flocked to make the five-star hotels by the Nile River in Cairo their temporary playground.

Taxi drivers, shopkeepers, street vendors, and almost everyone else who came into contact with the Kuwaiti exiles said they had flaunted their money, abused traditional Arab hospitality, and acted as if the war was a holiday.

"They have spent all their time in the discos while Egyptians are dying in the battlefield," one Egyptian was quoted as saying. "Our country is getting poorer every day, so how much compassion should I feel?"

Egyptian Gazette columnist Hassan Kamy wrote that Egyptians were being treated as "second-class citizens" in their own country.

"Discos of our capital, for instance, are the stage of a frantic activity of those guests of ours," he wrote. "Dressed up to the nines, perfumed with much lack of taste, our 'friends' are there, to spend noisy joyful hours of savage dancing and more savage spending, with no apparent concern whatsoever towards what happens to their homeland."

Such resentment is nothing new, however. People in the poorer Arab states have long felt that the oil-rich Persian Gulf Arabs have ignored their less-fortunate neighbors and hoarded their incredible wealth.

It was widely reported that after a spate of newspaper stories about disco-hopping Kuwaitis embarrassed the country's officials, they passed the word among the exiles to avoid the late-night scene.

But the warning apparently didn't faze Benal Amani, who reportedly spent every night at the same casino in an exclusive hotel.

"You probably think badly of me because I am not at the front," he was quoted as telling an American at the blackjack table. "But I have asthma, so I cannot fight. Otherwise, I would be there."

Not surprisingly, many had trouble believing that. But such stories didn't seem to sink in with Americans. Thanks to the propaganda, the linguistic legerdemain, the public-relations prevarications, the marketing manipulations, and a great victory over a second-rate army of a Third World nation run by a brutal fool, columnist Georgie Ann Geyer's assessment that the press was one of the conflict's biggest losers was close to being true.

Even the newly elected national president of the American Civil Liberties Union seemed to agree. Two days after the cease-fire took effect, Nadine Strossen, a professor of constitutional law at New York Law School, said the American tradition of free speech and a free press had taken a battering during the war.

"The legacy of the free speech restrictions that have been imposed and unfortunately widely accepted during this war will stay with us," she said during a speech to the Cleveland City Club.

Strossen, who stressed that the ACLU takes no position for or against wars, nonetheless insisted "that the government, in times of peace as well as in times of war, respect the rights of the American people."

She said creation of press pools, censorship of news reports, and military escorts for reporters in the field all contributed to the way in which the war was perceived.

"Even if the military escort does not literally interrupt an interview, of course you can understand that his or her presence has a chilling effect on the interview process," she said.

All of this would undoubtedly please Orwell's Big Brother. But it would greatly distress America's Founding Fathers.

"If I had to choose between a government and no press or a free press and no government, I would choose the latter," wrote Thomas Jefferson.

The reason, Jefferson said, was that "to the press alone, chequered as it is with abuses, the world is indebted for the triumphs which have been gained by reason and humanity over error and oppression. Jefferson's protégé, Bill of Rights author James Madison, echoed that belief when he wrote: "A popular government without popular information, or the means to acquire it, is but a prologue to a farce or a tragedy, or perhaps both."

And that, history may ultimately show, was exactly the legacy of the war in the Persian Gulf.

For, as the following chapters will detail, this was a war of devious deception more than of passionate principle.

It came about after a steady, inexplicable inflation of demands and expectations, each being used to justify the next. And then, in a decision made before congressional elections but not announced until afterward, a doubling of forces turned a defensive deployment into an offensive one with quite different goals and demands.

How did this horrific crisis, which eventually cost tens of thousands of lives, come about?

To answer that, we must go back to the beginning—not the beginning of the crisis, but to the beginning of history itself, in the "cradle of civilization," a nation we now call Iraq.

Rocking the Cradle

Iraq has a long and proud history. It also has a violent and bloody one. Those contradictory influences in the "cradle of civilization" have caused complications since the beginning of recorded time.

It was in Iraq that cities first flourished, the written word first appeared, the first legal code was promulgated, the system of time was first devised, modern mathematics was first used, the first school for astronomers was established—and the first wars were fought.

Ages before oil became what made the world go 'round, Iraq was both strategically and economically important. Although it is surrounded by desert, Iraq is sustained by two navigable rivers of immense historical importance—the Tigris and the Euphrates. Through irrigation, the two rivers provided fertile crops and a transportation route for roaming tribes and attackers as long ago as 3500 B.C.

The first civilization in Iraq was that of the Sumerians, who developed the world's first urban culture, writing system, and governmental bureaucracy in the plains south of modern Baghdad around 3000 B.C.

A millennium later, two great civilizations sprang up in the area between the Tigris and the Euphrates, which the Greeks called Mesopotamia.

To the north were the Assyrians, who developed the world's first militaristic culture. (Modern-day Assyrians, ironically, were a Christian minority whose men complained of being forced to join the Iraqi army, then being kept in it for years against their will.)

To the south were the enlightened Babylonians, who developed the modern system of time and much more. Babylon reached its peak in the sixth century B.C. during the rule of Nebuchadnezzar, to whom Saddam Hussein has often compared himself. It is easy to see why: Not only did Babylon prosper under Nebuchadnezzar, but he drove the Egyptians out of what is now Iraq and later expanded his territory by destroying Judah and Jerusalem.

But Babylon, like most great civilizations, had overextended itself, and soon collapsed from within. Around 500 B.C., both Babylon and Assyria were conquered by Cyrus the Great of Persia. In the coming centuries, the Greeks, Romans, Persians, Turks, and British all came to dominate the area.

Those who stayed the longest were the Ottoman Turks, who controlled most of the Mideast from the fifteenth to the twentieth centuries.

Unfortunately, the Ottomans made the mistake of fighting on the side of the losing Axis Powers in World War I. Britain took advantage of that by targeting Iraq for conquest in 1914. The British saw the region as a strategic jewel because of its position as a route to India, and because of its presumed oil reserves. Oil was of critical importance to Britain, whose huge navy had just begun using it in place of coal. Britain's first attempt at conquering Baghdad was a fiasco, however; thirteen thousand British troops were forced to surrender, and at least seven thousand of them died in captivity. But the British weren't about to give up, and Baghdad was finally captured in 1917.

To the Victors Go the Spoils

In the aftermath of World War I, the Ottoman Empire's Mideast territory was seized by Britain and France under the terms of the Sykes-Picot Agreement. The two victors created a system of "mandates," a euphemism for colonies, which they were to lead to independence under the supervision of the short-lived League of Nations.

Under this arrangement, France got the mandates of Lebanon and Syria, and the British got Iraq, Palestine, and Transjordan, which later became Jordan.

This development probably delighted Lord Curzon, the viceroy of India from 1899 to 1905, who had defined the provinces some time before as "the pieces on the chessboard upon which is being played out a game for the domination of the world."

Recognizing this—and that Kuwait had the best natural harbor in the Persian Gulf, making it the entry point for trade between Baghdad and India—the British in 1899 had signed a friendship treaty with a member of the Sabah family, which had ruled Kuwait for nearly 150 years. Under terms of the treaty, the Sabahs ran Kuwait's internal affairs but Britain was in charge of the tiny land's defense and foreign relations. This agreement was ratified in a 1913 pact with the Ottoman Empire.

Britain had further sown the seeds for its takeover of the area after World War I by forming an alliance with Sharif Hussein of Mecca. Hussein was head of the Hashemites, a clan that traced its origins to Muhammad, the prophet of Islam. T. E. Lawrence, whose exploits were glamorized in David Lean's 1962 film *Lawrence of Arabia,* promised Hussein that the British would support the formation of an independent Arab state stretching from the Persian Gulf to the Mediterranean Sea in return for his leadership of an Arab revolt against the Turks.

The British then proceeded in their usual fashion to make a

royal mess of the region. When Sharif Hussein refused to accept
the postwar treaties because they didn't fulfill Lawrence's promises,
the British encouraged a rival clan led by Abdul Aziz Ibn Saud
to overthrow Hussein in 1924. In 1932, Saud created the kingdom
of Saudi Arabia, which is now ruled by his eleventh son, King Fahd.

To soothe hard feelings and quell violent anti-British riots,
however, the British installed Sharif Hussein's son Faisal as king
of Iraq and his son Abdallah as king of Transjordan. Although
the Hashemite monarchy in Iraq was overthrown in 1958, it survives
to this day in Jordan under King Hussein Ibn Talal, the great-
grandson of Sharif Hussein.

During Britain's repressive rule of Iraq in the 1920s, the Royal
Air Force established a precedent for Saddam Hussein's later attacks
on the rebellious Kurds by destroying entire villages with bombs.
Some of those bombs were even designed to detonate after the
return of any Kurds who had managed to flee before an attack.

When the British High Commissioner for Iraq, Sir Percy Cox,
delineated the borders for the mandates in 1922, he went out of
his way to reward Britain's cooperative friends in Kuwait and to
limit the rebellious Iraqis' influence in the gulf.

As a result, tiny Kuwait was granted part of what had been
considered Iraqi territory, as well as a 310-mile coastline with several
deep-water ports. Iraq, on the other hand, was given a mere 36
miles of coastline and a major deep-water port, which it had to
share with Iran.

As drawn up by the British, the mandate of Iraq was actually
a blend of three Ottoman provinces. In the north was Mosul, which
was dominated by non-Arabic Kurds, who are generally members
of the dominant Sunni Muslim sect. In the center was Baghdad,
which was dominated by Arabic Sunni Muslims. In the more
populous south was Basra, which was predominantly populated
by Arabic Shiite Muslims.

King Faisal, who was a Sunni, expressed the same frustrations during his reign over these diverse peoples that Saddam Hussein would no doubt feel sixty years later:

> This government rules over a Kurdish group who call upon [Kurds] to abandon the government because it is not of their race. It also rules a Shiite plurality which belongs to the same ethnic group as the government. But as a result of the discriminations which the Shiites incurred under Ottoman rule, which did not allow them to participate in the affairs of the government, a wide breach developed between these two sects. . . . There are also other huge blocks of tribes . . . who want to reject everything related to the government because of their interests and the ambitions of their sheiks. . . . I say with my heart full of sadness that there is not yet in Iraq an Iraqi people.

Within a year of gaining its independence in 1932, Iraq, under its new king, Ghazi, tried to annex Kuwait. But Britain thwarted that attempt, as it would find itself helping others to do two more times by 1990.

Shortly after Iraq's Hashemite monarchy was overthrown in a July 14, 1958, military coup led by Gen. Abdul Karin Qassim, discussions on the border dispute were held with the emir of Kuwait, though little progress was made.

When Kuwait proclaimed its independence from Britain on June 19, 1961, Qassim congratulated the emir for abrogating the 1899 Anglo-Kuwaiti Security Agreement, but refused to recognize Kuwait as an independent state.

A week later, in a move that foreshadowed the one that would create a major international crisis three decades later, Iraq threatened to invade Kuwait. Egypt's Gamal Abdel Nasser, who saw Qassim as a potential rival for Arab loyalties, publicly supported the Sabah monarchy, and Britain and Saudi Arabia sent troops to Kuwait to help the newly independent nation defend its disputed border.

On February 8, 1963, Qassim was overthrown by a revolutionary council dominated by the Pan-Arabist Baath Party of Ahmad Hassan Bakr but headed by nationalist Abd al-Salim Arif.

According to some critics of U.S. policy, the CIA had collaborated with those behind the coup and had provided them with the names of Iraqi communists, who were quickly eliminated.

Arif soon announced a desire to resolve the border dispute with Kuwait, and Saudi Arabia took the initiative to broker a watershed agreement in which Baghdad, in return for a large payment from the Sabah monarchy, recognized Kuwait's "independence and total sovereignty."

Or so it was thought. As it turned out, the two governments still could not resolve their dispute over ownership of the fifty-mile-long Rumalia oilfield, a small part of which extended from Iraq into Kuwait, and Kuwait's Bubiyan and Warbah islands, which blocked Iraq's only outlet to the Persian Gulf through the Shatt al-Arab estuary.

When the fourth coup in ten years eliminated Arif in 1968, Bakr became president and quickly renewed Iraq's claim on Kuwait. Eventually, Baghdad gained the right to station forces in Kuwaiti territory as it confronted Iran over control of Shatt al-Arab. A young but already ruthless Saddam Hussein, then vice president and a member of the Revolutionary Command Council, acknowledged past errors and pledged Iraq's cooperation with all gulf countries other than Iran.

In 1975, Hussein went a step further and proposed a compromise stipulating that Kuwait lease to Iraq, for a duration of ninety-nine years, half of Bubiyan Island and surrender Warbah. In return, Iraq would recognize the existing borders between the two nations. Kuwait considered the proposal an insult and rejected it.

Hussein Takes Command

The situation changed in 1979 with the rise of the Ayatollah Khomeini in Iran and Hussein in Iraq. With the support of Kuwait, Saudi Arabia, and other moderate gulf states, all of which feared the spread of Khomeini's Islamic fundamentalism and military power, Iraq invaded Iran in 1980, ostensibly over the Shatt al-Arab dispute. According to a story in London's respected *Financial Times,* the United States had also encouraged Iraq's invasion by providing Hussein, through third-party Arab governments, intelligence and satellite data indicating that Iranian forces would crack quickly if attacked.

As the war progressed, Hussein insisted that the need to build a naval base on Bubiyan Island was critical, and reiterated his demand for a ninety-nine-year lease. But Kuwait still balked, even though it was facilitating the transfer of goods to Iraq through its ports. When it appeared that Iran was about to attack Warbah and Bubiyan, Kuwait placed its own forces on the strategically important islands and declared them military zones.

But that didn't deter Tehran. In March 1988, Iranian forces attacked several military installations on Bubiyan Island and injured a number of Kuwaiti soldiers. These attacks took place two years after Iran had seized the Faw Peninsula, the loss of which Baghdad blamed on a lack of defensive positions that Iraqi bases on Bubiyan would have provided. Iraq eventually retook Faw, but Hussein reportedly never forgave Kuwait for the tremendous losses it took to do so.

It is important to note that the United States didn't denounce Iraq's unprovoked aggression in this instance. Instead, with the exception of the ill-fated shipment of missiles to Tehran as part of the Iran-contra scandal, it actively supported Iraq by providing military intelligence, huge shipments of agricultural goods, and under-the-table transfers of military materiel. The reason was simple:

The Iranian seizure of American hostages in 1979 remained a source of yellow-ribbon outrage among Americans long after the hostages' release in January 1981.

But diplomatic relations between the United States and Iraq had been broken after the Arab-Israeli war of 1967, and their reestablishment was delayed when on June 1, 1981, Israel attacked the Osirak nuclear reactor outside Baghdad to destroy Iraq's ability to develop nuclear weapons. Although the United States denounced the unprovoked attack, its close relationship with Israel temporarily foiled chances of developing relations with Baghdad. The attack also had a long-term impact on Hussein's attitude toward Israel: He was determined to avenge the humiliation, and finally did so, ten years later.

The military situation grew even worse for Hussein in 1982, when Iran repelled a major Iraqi offensive. That raised concern in the United States that Iran would win the war, and the Reagan administration decided to quietly come to Iraq's aid. The increasingly friendly relationship became more open in 1984, when the United States officially established diplomatic relations with Baghdad. Starting a year later, the United States began supplying Iraq with important military intelligence that helped Hussein to turn the tide against Iran.

Also starting in 1985, the Reagan administration began the approval of what by 1990 totaled $1.5 billion in sales of advanced U.S. products to Iraq.

Records made available in early March 1991 to the House Government Operations Committee's subcommittee on commerce, consumer, and monetary affairs revealed that the U.S. government approved 771 sales of high technology to Iraq. According to the *Washington Post,* the purchases included "advanced computers, radio equipment, graphics terminals that could be used to design rockets and analyze their flights, machine tools, computer mapping systems and imaging devices for reading satellite pictures."

The *Post* said Pentagon war reports showed that much of the technology was sold to the Iraqi Defense Ministry, the Interior Ministry, and the Atomic Energy Commission, as well as to universities and scientific institutions that were later bombed by coalition forces for being part of Iraq's poison gas and nuclear weapons establishment.

According to the *Los Angeles Times,* U.S. helicopters worth $25 million that were sold to Iraq, allegedly for crop dusting, were used to attack Kurdish civilians in 1988. The United States also authorized the sale of sixteen helicopters, at a cost of $39 million, to the Iraqi air force for search-and-rescue operations.

Although the sales were started to aid Iraq's war against Iran, they continued after the war's conclusion in an effort to encourage Hussein to be a more responsible member of the international community and a stabilizing force in the Mideast.

This policy continued unabated even after an Iraqi warplane severely damaged the *USS Stark* and killed thirty-seven U.S. sailors in an Exocet missile attack in 1987. Instead of being outraged, both the American public and its government accepted Iraq's claim that the attack was an accident.

The *Washington Post* said the trade records turned over to Congress showed that in the fifteen days preceding Iraq's August 2 invasion of Kuwait, the Bush administration approved licenses for $4.8 million in advanced-technology products. The policy continued right up until the day before Iraq invaded Kuwait, when the Bush administration approved the sale of $695,000 worth of advanced data-transmission devices.

The generous policy toward Iraq extended to other areas, as well. On December 20, 1989, the White House announced that it was lifting the ban on loans to Iraq. A few weeks later, the State Department said that "the goal of increasing U.S. exports puts us in a better position to deal with Iraq regarding its human-rights record." At the time of the invasion, Iraq was the world's leading recipient of U.S.-subsidized grain sales, even though there was ample evidence that some of the agricultural subsidies were being used to buy military equipment.

"What it means is the administration had no problem with Iraq until the day after Saddam's troops walked into Kuwait," the *Post* quoted an administration official as saying.

But the United States was hardly alone in its permissive trading policies with Iraq. One of the biggest ironies of the Persian Gulf War, in fact, was that many of the nations that fought to dismantle Hussein's "military machine" were the same ones that had helped to build it. Among the culprits were:

• The Soviet Union, which the Stockholm International Peace Research Institute says supplied 53 percent of the conventional weapons Iraq bought during the 1980s.

• France, which supplied 20 percent of Hussein's imported weapons, including about one hundred sophisticated F-1 jet fighters armed with France's effective Exocet missiles. The French also supplied Iraq with point-defense radar, Puma helicopters, and the camouflage nets and weapon decoys that initially confused coalition pilots during the Persian Gulf War.

• Germany, whose firms sold Iraq technology and expertise used to develop, among other things, chemical weapons.

• China, which provided up to 10 percent of Iraq's weaponry.

• South Africa, which provided Baghdad with two hundred of its deadly howitzers. The South African government denied reports during the war that ARMSCOR, its arms-making unit, had sold Iraq its entire 1990 production of special G-5 155mm artillery ammunition, including some poison-gas shells.

• Egypt, which sold Hussein many of his Soviet-built tanks and artillery pieces and even permitted thousands of its citizens to join the Iraqi Army.

• Belgium, whose engineers designed Iraq's underground aircraft shelters.

Iraqi President Saddam Hussein appears on a videotaped message to the American people, promising President Bush that he was sending his citizens to a war "more terrible than Vietnam." *(AP/Wide World Photos)*

Peter Arnett: The only American television journalist who reported from Baghdad throughout the entire war. (*CNN*)

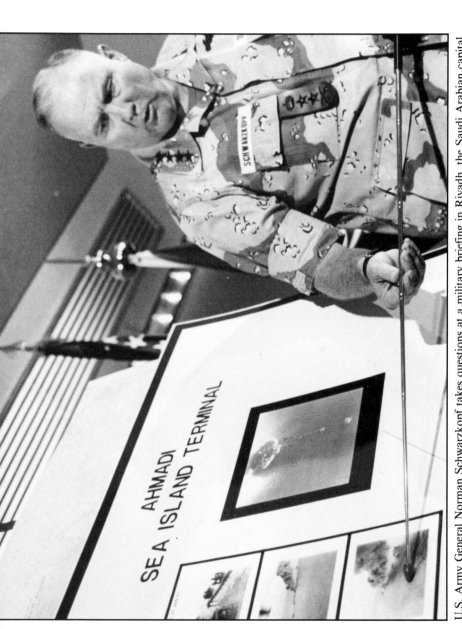

U.S. Army General Norman Schwarzkopf takes questions at a military briefing in Riyadh, the Saudi Arabian capital. Schwarzkopf's television demeanor, carefully crafted, was a key ingredient in the marketing of Desert Storm.

(*AP/Wide World Photos*)

"The Road to Baghdad." Accurate casualty figures will probably never be known.

(AP/Wide World Photos)

- Switzerland, which provided the shelters' air-filtration systems.
- Italy, which supplied the shelters' doors and many of the Iraqi army's mines.
- Britain, which provided the shelters' power generators, as well as sophisticated radar systems.

Nor did the U.N.-mandated embargo on trade with Iraq stop Hussein from procuring many of the supplies he needed to keep his military machine running.

Between August, when the embargo went into effect, and early February, Western intelligence and law-enforcement officials said they had detected more than eight hundred attempts to sell Iraq everything from apples to ammunition.

Officials in Germany's Economics Ministry were quoted in March news reports as saying that up to 110 German firms had broken the embargo. They said nine were under criminal investigation at that time.

Jordan remained the most common smuggling route despite the round-the-clock bombing during the war of the road between Baghdad and Amman.

To the Victor Goes the Toils

When the Iran-Iraq War petered out in 1988, with little accomplished by either side save the accumulation of a million casualties between them, Hussein still emerged an Arab hero. Not only had Iran, with fifty-five million people to Iraq's eighteen million, cried "uncle" first, Hussein's Arab supporters argued, but Islamic fundamentalism also had been greatly stifled.

But Iraq had paid a horrible price to make Hussein a hero. Although Iraq still abounded in oil—its hundred billion barrels put it second only to Saudi Arabia in proven reserves—the Iraqi economy and infrastructure had been devastated during the war, and domestic political discontent had risen so high that there had been assassination attempts on Hussein in 1989 and early 1990.

The war also left the country $80 billion in debt. As a result, an increasingly uneasy Hussein began to look for a scapegoat. Kuwait made a convenient target because of its longstanding border dispute with Iraq and its denial of the use of Warbah and Bubiyan.

The closer Hussein looked, listened, and calculated, the more he thought he had reason to get angry.

According to the October 21 issue of Britain's *Sunday Observer,* he also had some help in this process from a most unlikely source—the United States, which the paper said, "actively encouraged . . . Hussein to pursue an aggressive policy of higher oil prices seven months before the invasion of Kuwait."

The newspaper quoted high-level U.S. sources as saying it was "discreetly suggested" by a former U.S. ambassador with close ties to the Bush administration, in a January 1990 meeting with a top Iraqi official, that Saddam threaten force if necessary to coerce Kuwait to increase oil prices. The *Sunday Observer* said that, because of declining oil prices primarily caused by Kuwaiti over-production, Hussein was facing a $7 billion shortfall that year, a $100 billion foreign debt, and the demobilization of several hundred thousand troops, with few jobs for them to come back to. It added that higher prices would also aid the sagging oil-based economy in Bush's home state of Texas, as well as those of Louisiana, Alaska, and Arizona by making U.S. oil more competitive.

The newspaper said that Bush's envoy had referred Hussein to a prominent Washington think tank, the Center for Strategic and International Studies, to help him devise an economic rescue operation. Though specific recommendations remained secret, the paper said they were reflected in an interview with G. Henry M. Schuler, the center's director of energy-security programs, that appeared in the March 1, 1990, issue of the *Arab Oil & Gas Journal.*

In the interview, Schuler said the Persian Gulf oil exporting states would be able to get up to $25 a barrel (almost $10 a barrel higher than the going rate at the time) if a price policy was pushed by a nation "with the power to force all the states in the gulf to follow suit."

But Schuler strongly—and convincingly—denied that he or his think tank devised such a strategy for Iraq. "I don't know about any meeting between an ex-ambassador and Iraq, but I can deny categorically that I did any such study," Schuler said in an interview with the author. "When I said that to the *Arab Oil & Gas Journal,* I was actually thinking of Saudi Arabia, not Iraq."

He added, however, that, "the oil dimension of this crisis has been totally ignored, and it needs to be understood."

Schuler, in fact, raised several interesting points about the Iraq-Kuwait dispute in a *Los Angeles Times* commentary on December 2, 1990. Among them:

• Kuwait had been making increasingly aggressive incursions into a buffer zone established between the two nations as a temporary solution to their long-standing border dispute.

• The emirate had been stealing Iraqi oil by slant-drilling in the buffer zone, which, in addition to providing revenue, reinforced Kuwait's claim to the disputed area.

• Kuwait refused to wipe off the books money it had given Iraq out of the huge windfall Kuwait had reaped by supplying Iraq's oil customers during the war with Iran—which had been waged partly at Kuwait's urging.

• In October, Iraq released a document it said was found in Kuwait's Foreign Ministry files that reported on a week of meetings between Kuwaiti and U.S. officials, including CIA Director William Webster, in November 1989. The document stated, "We agreed with the American side that it was important to take advantage of the deteriorating economic structure in Iraq in order to put pressure on that country's government to delineate our common border." Schuler said the CIA has admitted that Webster met with senior Kuwaiti officials on the date specified in the document, but claimed that it was a "routine courtesy call." The agency said that nothing about Kuwait's relations with Iraq had been mentioned "at that meeting," which appeared to leave open the possibility that the subject had been discussed at other meetings.

Schuler urged Congress to ask the questions these points raised, "even though we might not like the answers." After some initial interest from Congress to do so, Schuler said, the issue was dropped amid the euphoric reaction to the war's successful execution and conclusion. Some stones apparently were then deemed better left unturned.

Yet the purported Kuwaiti document did add considerable credence to Jordan's contention that the crisis could have been caused by a U.S.-Kuwaiti scheme that backfired.

As reported by Milton Viorst in the January 7, 1991, issue of the *New Yorker,* Crown Prince Hassan, King Hussein's younger brother, claimed that most Arabs found Kuwait's defiance toward Iraq in the months leading up to the invasion "incomprehensible." Kuwait's overproduction, he told Viorst, had forced the price of oil well below OPEC's target, to the great detriment of Iraq, and to a lesser extent to Saudi Arabia, more than to Kuwait itself.

Kuwait had learned during the Iran-Iraq War how overproduction had helped bring Iran to its knees by cutting its oil profits when they were most needed. According to Viorst, some analysts wondered whether Kuwait was now trying the same strategy against Iraq—perhaps with Washington's tacit approval.

Meanwhile, the Bush administration had begun a series of verbal assaults on Iraq for its previously overlooked reported gassing of the Kurds, construction of a "supercannon," and its foiled efforts to obtain triggering devices for nuclear weapons.

Soon, talk of imminent warfare began making the rounds in Israel, much as it had on the eve of its 1981 bombing of Iraq's nuclear facility.

This supposedly frightened Hussein enough that he made his much-publicized threat to retaliate with chemical weapons if Israel ever attacked Iraq again. That further fueled anti-Iraqi feelings in the United States, to the point that King Hussein felt compelled to decry the "unholy campaign against Iraq" during an Arab summit in Baghdad.

"We didn't know what it all meant," Viorst quoted one royal adviser as saying about this strange series of events. "We couldn't put together the pieces of the mosaic, but we were suspicious." Coincidentally, Iraq was making plans to construct a naval base at Umm Qasr on its narrow gulf coastline that would be linked by a deep-water canal to Basra. But the new harbor would require control of the long-disputed Kuwaiti islands of Bubiyan and Warbah to provide for the base's security.

Viorst said this was supposedly seen as a threat to American plans to station a larger naval force in the gulf, which the United States needed to control the flow of oil there.

"Kuwait, because it owned the islands, played an inordinately important role in this shadow struggle," Viorst wrote. "During a series of diplomatic encounters throughout the spring and summer, the Kuwaitis took an extremely hard line with Iraq. The Iraqi position is that Kuwait offered no concessions, either on oil production limits or on control of the islands or on the possession of Rumalia oil fields."

Instead, Kuwait reportedly continued to ask for repayment, with interest, of the disputed "loans" it had made to Iraq during war with Iran.

"The Kuwaitis were very cocky," Viorst quoted one of King Hussein's aides as saying. "They told us officially that the United States would intervene if there was trouble with Iraq"—but only, it appears, after U.S. and Kuwaiti officials ignored warnings that Saddam Hussein's threats were serious.

Shortly after the Gulf War had ended, for example, a former

diplomat in Kuwait's consulate in Basra said his government had ignored his warnings that Iraq would invade on August 2. According to *USA Today,* Kuwaiti officials abruptly ended a news conference in Kuwait City as Col. Matar aid Matar was about to elaborate on his statement that he had reported the invasion plan to his superiors on July 25.

At any rate, King Hussein claims the crisis still could have been defused after the invasion, if the United States had wanted it to be. As evidence, he notes that Saudi Arabia's King Fahd originally expressed no fear of an Iraqi invasion and even proposed that Iraq withdraw to the disputed border area, giving it control of the Rumailia oil fields and the two important islands.

When President Bush announced on August 8 that he was sending U.S. troops to defend Saudi Arabia, Viorst noted, Iraq said it had already informed the U.S. embassy in Baghdad that it had no intention of invading Saudi territory.

Viorst said that King Hussein later was told the same thing by Saddam Hussein himself, who had added that he had invaded Kuwait to teach it a lesson and planned to withdraw that coming weekend as long as it didn't appear he was being forced to. According to Viorst, the king then arranged an Arab summit to allow the two nations' leaders to work out their differences. But Kuwait changed its mind. It appealed to the United Nations for a motion demanding Iraqi withdrawal, and quickly received one. Egyptian President Hosni Mubarak further complicated matters by denouncing the invasion later that day. When King Hussein called to ask why he had done so rather than go through with the Arab summit, Mubarak reportedly replied that he was "under tremendous pressure."

When the Arab League followed the U.N. lead and condemned the invasion that same day, a furious Saddam Hussein withdrew his promise to attend an Arab summit. Bush then proceeded to rapidly assemble his coalition, and the line was about to be drawn in the sand.

Although they said they had no hard evidence, King Hussein's aides told Viorst they wondered whether a war aimed at the destruction of Iraq—or at least its war-making potential—had been the U.S. goal all along.

"It seems to us that the position of the Americans has been war, war, war from the very beginning," Crown Prince Hassan said.

If so, Saddam Hussein had begun to take the bait in May 1990, when he took the verbal offensive at the Arab League summit in Baghdad by declaring Kuwait's policy "economic warfare."

In addition to a change in Kuwaiti oil policies, Hussein demanded $27 billion in reparations.

Kuwaiti officials replied that there was no way they could meet his monetary demands, but they would reconsider their production policy.

On July 10, under pressure from Saudi Arabia and Iran as well as Iraq, Kuwait and the United Arab Emirates agreed at a special OPEC meeting to abide by the cartel's production quotas. But that was no longer enough for Saddam Hussein. He continued to make demands for cash. Kuwait still balked.

In response, Hussein began deploying more and more troops along the Kuwaiti border.

Then, on July 25, Hussein summoned April Glaspie, the U.S. ambassador to Baghdad, to his office on one hour's notice, for "comprehensive political discussions."

An Iraqi transcript of their dialogue, which was not disputed by Glaspie until eight months later, showed, if nothing else, how easily Hussein could have misread U.S. intentions.

Hussein began the meeting with a long-winded review of the region's problems, most of which he traced to its colonial period. He then moved on to U.S.-Iraqi relations, noting that he had accepted an American apology for the "Irangate" fiasco, during which the United States had sold weapons to Iran, and "wiped the slate clean."

He also expressed "suspicions" about whether the United States had been pleased with the war's outcome, then referred to the current crisis:

> Iraq came out of the war burdened with $40 billion in debts, excluding the aid given by Arab states, some of whom consider that too to be a debt although they knew—and you knew too—that without Iraq they would not have had these sums and the future of the region would have been entirely different.
>
> We began to face the policy of the drop in the price of oil. Then we saw the United States, which always talks of democracy but which has no time for the other point of view. Then the media campaign against Saddam Hussein was started by the official American media. [Hussein was referring to a February "Voice of America" editorial on secret police forces that depicted Iraq as one of several countries whose rulers "hold power by force and fear, not by the consent of the governed."] The United States thought that the situation in Iraq was like Poland, Romania, or Czechoslovakia. We were disturbed by this campaign, but we were not disturbed too much because we had hoped that, in a few months, those who are decision-makers in America would have a chance to find the facts and see whether this media campaign had any effect on the lives of Iraqis. We had hoped that soon the American authorities would make the correct decision regarding their relations with Iraq. Those with good relations can sometimes afford to disagree.
>
> But when planned and deliberate policy forces the price of oil down without good commercial reasons, then that means another war against Iraq. Because military war kills people by bleeding them, and economic war kills their humanity by depriving them of their chance to have a good standard of living. As you know, we gave rivers of blood in a war that lasted eight years, but we did not lose our humanity. Iraqis have a right to live proudly. We do not accept that anyone could injure Iraqi pride or the Iraqi right to have high standards of living.

Kuwait and the UAE were at the front of this policy aimed at lowering Iraq's position and depriving its people of higher economic conditions. On top of all that, while we were busy at war, the state of Kuwait began to expand at the expense of our territory.

You may say this is propaganda, but I would direct you to one document, [the one establishing the] Military Patrol Line, which is the border line endorsed by the Arab League in 1961 for military patrols not to cross the Iraq-Kuwait border. But go and look for yourselves. You will see the Kuwaiti border patrols, the Kuwaiti farms, the Kuwaiti oil installations—all built as closely as possible to this line to establish that land as Kuwaiti territory. . . . So what can it mean when America says it will now protect its friends? It can only mean prejudice against Iraq. This stance plus maneuvers and statements which have been made has encouraged the UAE and Kuwait to disregard Iraqi rights.

I say to you clearly, that Iraq's rights, which are mentioned in the memorandum, we will take one by one. That might not happen now or after a month or after a year, but we will take it all. We are not the kind of people who will relinquish their rights. There is no historic right, or legitimacy, or need for the UAE and Kuwait to deprive us of our rights. If they are needy, we are needy too.

The United States must have a better understanding of the situation and declare who it wants to have relations with and who its enemies are. But it should not make enemies simply because others have different points of view regarding the Arab-Israeli conflict.

You are appeasing the usurper [Israel] in so many ways—economically, politically, and militarily, as well as in the media. When will the time come when, for every three appeasements to the usurper, you praise the Arabs just once?

"I clearly understand your message," Glaspie replied. "We studied history at school. They taught us to say freedom or death.

I think you know well that we as a people have our experience with the colonialists."

Glaspie went on to relate that President Bush opposed congressional efforts to implement trade sanctions in protest of Iraq's human-rights record.

She continued: "I have a direct instruction from the president to seek better relations with Iraq."

Hussein: "But how? We, too, have this desire. But matters are running contrary to this desire."

Glaspie: "This is less likely to happen the more we talk. For example, you mentioned the issue of the article published by the American Information Agency, and that was sad, and a formal apology was presented."

Hussein: "Your stance is generous. . . . But the media campaign continued. And it is full of stories. If the stories were true, no one would get upset. But we understand from its continuation that there is a determination [to attack Iraq]."

Glaspie continued:

I saw the Diane Sawyer program on ABC. And what happened in that program was cheap and unjust. And this is a real picture of what happens in the American media—even to American politicians themselves. These are the methods the Western media employ. I am pleased that you add your voice to the diplomats who stand up to the media. Because your appearance in the media, even for five minutes, would help us make the American people understand Iraq. This would increase mutual understanding. If the American president had control of the media, his job would be much easier.

Mr. President, not only do I want to say that President Bush wants better and deeper relations with Iraq, but he also wants an Iraqi contribution to peace and prosperity in the Middle East. . . .

You are right. It is true what you say that we do not want

higher prices for oil. But I would ask you to examine the possibility of not charging too high a price for oil.

"We do not want too high a price for oil," Hussein said. "Twenty-five dollars is not a high price. The price at one stage had dropped to $12 a barrel and reduction in the modest Iraqi budget of $6 billion to $7 billion is a disaster."

And then came a comment from Glaspie that would be widely quoted during and after the Persian Gulf War:

"I think I understand this," she said. "I have lived here for years. I admire your extraordinary efforts to rebuild your country. I know you need funds. We understand that and our opinion is that you should have the opportunity to rebuild your country. But we have no opinion on the Arab-Arab conflicts, like your border disagreement with Kuwait."

April Glaspie's War?

Critics said that comment might have signaled a green light for Hussein to invade Kuwait a week later. Glaspie was harshly criticized by many member of Congress, and a good number still contend that Bush's policy toward Iraq was misdirected and that Glaspie, on orders or alone, triggered events that led to the costly war.

For example, Sen. Patrick Leahy, a Vermont Democrat, told National Public Radio that the battle to liberate Kuwait would be remembered as "April Glaspie's war."

After arriving in Washington following Iraq's invasion of Kuwait, Glaspie was assigned to prepare papers on Mideast policy based on her experience serving in U.S. embassies in Tunisia, Syria, Egypt, Jordan, and Iraq.

On September 23, the *New York Times* reported that "interviews with dozens of administration officials, lawmakers and independent experts and a review of public statements and the Iraqi document show that instead of sending Mr. Hussein blunt messages through public and private statements that an invasion would be unacceptable, the State Department prepared equivocal statements for the administration about American commitments to Kuwait."

The *Times* said U.S. strategy was based on the assumption that Iraq wouldn't invade Kuwait, or, if it did, that Washington and most of the Arab world probably would accept a limited invasion in which Iraq seized parts of Kuwait to gain concessions.

"We were reluctant to draw a line in the sand," the *Times* quoted a senior administration official as saying. "I can't see the American public supporting the deployment of troops over a dispute over twenty miles of desert territory, and it is not clear that the local countries would have supported that kind of commitment. The basic principle is not to make threats you can't deliver on. That was one reason there was a certain degree of hedging on what was said."

After months of silence on Glaspie's statement, Secretary of State James A. Baker III finally said in February that Glaspie had not meant to signal approval for Hussein to invade Kuwait.

"I'm confident that she was not intending to give him the green light," Baker said in a CBS interview with Connie Chung.

Asked if events might have been different if Hussein had been "sufficiently warned, repeatedly warned in some way by the United States ambassador to Iraq," Baker replied, "Maybe, yes, absolutely. As the president has said, as I have said, with 20-20 hindsight, there might be some things we would have done differently."

But when Baker was asked if Glaspie had been expressing a policy that he had directed her to express, he replied with a simple no.

If that is the case, however, neither were two other top Baker aides who made statements similar to Glaspie's in the days immediately before the invasion.

On July 24, the day before Glaspie's meeting with Hussein, State Department spokeswoman Margaret Tutwiler was asked whether the United States had any commitment to defend Kuwait.

"We do not have any defense treaties with Kuwait, and there are no special defense or security commitments to Kuwait," she replied.

Asked if the United States would help Kuwait if it was attacked, Tutwiler replied, "We also remain strongly committed to supporting the individual and collective self-defense of our friends in the gulf with whom we have deep and longstanding ties"—a statement the *New York Times* quoted Kuwaiti officials as saying was too weak.

In her only public comment about her controversial meeting with Hussein, Glaspie seemed to give credence to the *Time*'s report that U.S. officials were prepared to accept a partial Iraqi invasion of Kuwait in order to gain concessions.

"I wish I had been the only one in the world who was right. Obviously I didn't think, and nobody else did, that the Iraqis were going to take all of Kuwait," Glaspie told the *New York Times* in September. "Every Kuwaiti and Saudi, every analyst in the Western world was wrong, too. That does not excuse me. But people who now claim that all was clear were not heard from at the time."

As detailed in a later chapter, Glaspie's story changed dramatically when she finally appeared (*performed* might be a more accurate term) before Congress.

At any rate, Hussein did assure Glaspie, as she later stressed, that there was no reason to be over-concerned. He said he still suspected that Kuwait would not honor any concessions it might agree to, but that negotiations were continuing and he had assured the Kuwaitis "that we are not going to do anything until we meet with them."

"When we meet and when we see that there is hope, then nothing will happen," he said. "But if we are unable to find a solution, then it will be natural that Iraq will not accept death. . . . There you have good news."

Good news has a strange way of turning into bad news, though, and it certainly did in this case. Hussein kept his promise that Iraq would meet with Kuwait before taking any further action. The meeting took place on July 31 in Jidda, Saudi Arabia. But no agreement was reached.

That same day, John H. Kelly, the assistant secretary of state for Near Eastern and South Asian affairs, told a congressional subcommittee: "We have no defense treaty relationships with any of the [gulf] countries. We have historically avoided taking a position on border disputes or on internal OPEC deliberations, but we have certainly, as have all administrations, resoundingly called for the peaceful settlement of disputes and differences in the region."

A week prior to that encouraging statement, Kelly's predecessor, Richard W. Murphy, had told the *International Herald Tribune* that comparisons of Hussein to Hitler were "too glib," and that the Iraqi dictator was merely "a rough, direct-talking leader."

At 2 A.M. on August 2, however, Hussein began talking with his tanks, which started rolling south. Six hours later, the Iraqis had annexed *all* of Kuwait, with its ninety billion barrels of oil. Even worse, their tanks were in a position to threaten Saudi Arabia's oilfields, with their 169 billion barrels.

Ironically, according to M. A. Adelman, a professor emeritus of economics at the Massachusetts Institute of Technology, Saudi Arabia had originally encouraged Iraq's threats of military action to cow Kuwait into falling in line with OPEC production guidelines. "As the cartel enforcer," Adelman wrote in *Foreign Policy* magazine, "Iraq succeeded in intimidating Kuwait, which agreed to cut production. But the cartel enforcer was thereby encouraged to hijack other OPEC members. The Saudis found their hired gun now pointed at them."

But the Saudis had an even bigger hired gun—as Saddam Hussein was about to find out.

The Bushkrieg

After doing little to dissuade Saddam Hussein from invading Kuwait, the United States answered Iraq's *blitzkrieg* with a *Bushkrieg* that was every bit as effective—and deceptive.

President Bush played it cool publicly when word reached Washington that Iraq's army had overrun Kuwait and seized the emir's palace and other government buildings, with hardly a fight from the Kuwaiti defense forces. But Bush was apparently seething privately. Bush, whose own Zapata Offshore Oil Co. had drilled the first well in the Persian Gulf off Kuwait thirty years earlier, had a personal appreciation for the emirate's value as a dependable source of cheap oil, on which the U.S. and other national economies had become so dependent. He undoubtedly also saw the invasion as a challenge to the United States' new role as the world's only "megapower," as conservatives had begun to call it.

So while Bush was still telling reporters that he was "not discussing intervention," he was telling his aides that "this must be reversed."

Later that day, Bush took his first action against the invasion, by ordering a U.S. economic embargo against Iraq.

Whatever doubts he may have had about his course of action

seemed to disappear after Bush visited Aspen, Colorado, where British Prime Minister Margaret Thatcher was staying at the mountain guest house of the U.S. ambassador to London, Henry Catto, during a private visit.

"He must be stopped," Thatcher reportedly told Bush during an impromptu two-hour meeting. Thatcher, who earned the nickname "The Iron Lady" and skyrocketing popularity for defeating the weak armed forces of Argentina in the 1982 Falklands War, told Bush that the only way to persuade Hussein to get out of her nation's former colony was by immediately sending troops.

Sir Anthony Acland, British ambassador to the United States, attended that meeting and diplomatically tried to play down Thatcher's role when asked about it by the author.

"I think it was comforting and reassuring for President Bush to learn that they were of the same mind," Acland said. "Mrs. Thatcher certainly reinforced his feelings, but I think he was headed in that direction anyway."

Regardless, it was during that meeting, a top aide was later quoted as saying, that Bush crossed the Rubicon. He decided to act—and act with authority. When Bush arrived back in Washington, he stated firmly that "this invasion will not stand."

According to *Newsweek*, Bush quickly convened the National Security Council to discuss American interests affected by the crisis. The main ones listed were the danger to oil supplies, Hussein's potential nuclear threat, the security of Israel, and the one that proved to be paramount—the threat to the United States' ability to control events now that it was the world's only superpower.

When Hussein sent his tanks into Kuwait, he had provided Bush with the perfect "defining moment," both for his presidency and for the shape of the post-Cold War world.

Bush's exaggerated portrayal of Hussein as another Hitler and his army as a massive military threat to world stability was no accident. Such a view served the political and foreign-policy objectives of an administration seeking to create Bush's "new world order" dominated by U.S. military power.

Michael Sherry, a professor of history at Northwestern University, was quoted as saying that this exaggerated view of Hussein and his army was not so much a failure of raw intelligence gathered by agents as it was "a political need to maximize the threat."

Another reason cited for overstating Hussein's power was that it would help to revitalize the defense budget and justify buying and building more high-tech weapons if they performed as expected in the Persian Gulf.

Perhaps with such considerations in mind, the Bush administration on August 6 took the first of a number of well-timed steps to build an international coalition against Iraq by persuading the U.N. Security Council to follow Bush's lead by ordering a worldwide embargo on trade with Iraq.

Telephone Diplomacy

Before the vote, Bush had begun phoning leaders around the world to mount a coalition against Hussein. As effective as Bush is supposed to be on the phone, however, the one leader he apparently never tried to engage in conversation during the seven-month crisis was Saddam Hussein. Such one-on-one contact, some analysts suggested, might have defused the crisis long before it came to war—just as direct communication between President Kennedy and Soviet leader Nikita Khrushchev proved crucial in resolving the Cuban missile crisis in 1962.

Also unlike Kennedy—who privately assured Khrushchev that the United States would withdraw some obsolete missiles from Turkey after the Soviet missiles were removed from Cuba, so the Soviet leader could make his concession look like part of a *quid pro quo* agreement—Bush refused to make the slightest face-saving gesture toward Hussein.

From the first day on, he chose confrontation over communication and controversy over compromise. The day after the U.N. vote, Bush drew his now-famous "line in the sand." He ordered deployment of U.S. combat troops, warplanes, and a Navy task force to Saudi Arabia as part of a "wholly defensive" mission to block what he said was an imminent Iraqi threat to Saudi Arabia and its vast oil reserves.

But many analysts now question whether Iraqi tanks were ever poised to roll into Saudi Arabia. Historians may someday compare this claim to the 1964 Gulf of Tonkin incident, in which a clash between U.S. destroyers and Vietnamese torpedo boats was apparently blown out of proportion by President Johnson in order to gain congressional authority to expand the Vietnam War.

Eugene Carroll, a retired U.S. Navy rear admiral with the private Center for Defense Information in Washington, told the *Toronto Globe and Mail* that Hussein had clearly hoped to absorb Kuwait.

"But in terms of passing through Kuwait and heading into Saudi Arabia, I see no evidence whatsoever that he had that in preparation," Carroll said.

The Bush administration created the issue, Carroll maintained, by "saying over and over again, 'He's going to take Saudi Arabia,' and who could question it? Who could doubt it? He's going to eat Saudi Arabia for breakfast.

"That's what the president said, and this became conventional wisdom, but please believe me, the White House has the power to create conventional wisdom."

Bush did exactly that on September 11, during an address to a joint session of Congress.

"We gather tonight, witness to events in the Persian Gulf as significant as they are tragic," Bush said. "In the early morning hours of August 2, following negotiations and promises by Iraq's dictator Saddam Hussein not to use force, a powerful Iraqi army invaded its trusting and much weaker neighbor, Kuwait. Within three days, one hundred and twenty thousand Iraqis with eight hundred and fifty tanks had poured into Kuwait and moved south to threaten Saudi Arabia. It was then I decided to act to check that aggression."

According to a January 6 article in the *St. Petersburg Times*, however, two American satellite imaging experts who examined two satellite photos taken the same day Bush delivered those words said the photos, which the paper had purchased for $1,560 each from a commercial Soviet service, failed to back up his claim, and showed no sign of a massive Iraqi troop buildup in Kuwait.

"The Pentagon kept saying the bad guys were there, but we don't see anything to indicate an Iraqi force in Kuwait of even 20 percent the size the administration claimed," Peter Zimmerman, who served with the U.S. Arms Control Disarmament Agency during the Reagan administration, told the newspaper.

What they could see, however, was the extensive U.S. military presence at the Dharan Airport in Saudi Arabia.

"We could see five C-141s, one C-5A and four smaller transport aircraft, probably C-130s," Zimmerman told *Times* Washington correspondent Jean Heller. "There is also a long line of fighters, F-111s or F-15s, on the ground. In the middle of the airfield are what could be camouflaged staging areas.

"We didn't find anything of that sort anywhere in Kuwait. We don't see any tent cities, we don't see congregations of tanks, we don't see troop concentrations, and the main Kuwaiti air base appears deserted. It's five weeks after the invasion, and from what we can see, the Iraqi air force hasn't flown a single fighter to the most strategic air base in Kuwait."

The Pentagon refused to explain the apparent discrepancy to the *Times*—or to Congress.

Rep. Charles Bennett of Jacksonville, Florida, the second-ranking Democrat on the House Armed Services Committee, told the *Times*: "We've had evidence in the sense that we've had testimony about what the situation was back in September, but I've seen no photographic evidence to back up the administration's claims."

Unfortunately, the national news media chose to ignore the *Times's* story.

According to *In These Times*, a liberal Chicago-based publication that reprinted the story, *St. Petersburg Times* editors approached the Associated Press twice about running the story, to no avail. They said the Scripps-Howard News Service, of which the paper is a member, also turned down the story.

Why?

"I think part of the reason the story was ignored was that it was published too close to the start of the war," Jean Heller told *In These Times*. "Second and most importantly, I don't think people wanted to hear that we might have been deceived. A lot of reporters who have seen the story think it is dynamite, but the editors who have seen it seem to have the attitude, 'At this point, who cares?' "

At that point, not many, thanks to Bush's clever manipulation of post-invasion events, in which he proved to have a willing accomplice in Saddam Hussein.

Dollar Diplomacy

Hussein's declaration on August 8 that Iraq had annexed Kuwait, for example, helped Bush to bring Britain into the multinational force he was assembling in the Persian Gulf.

Two days later, twelve of twenty Arab League states voted to send an all-Arab military force to join Bush's rapidly growing coalition. But the vote was by no means as supportive of Bush as it appeared. Six of the twelve members voting in favor were the small, pro-Western, oil-rich gulf monarchies—Kuwait, Saudi Arabia, Oman, Qatar, Bahrain, and the United Arab Emerits.

Lebanon's vote was controlled by Hussein's archenemy, Syrian dictator Hafez Assad. According to *Time* magazine, the Bush administration had earlier agreed to tolerate Assad's de facto takeover of Lebanon in return for his staying out of the Palestinian-Israeli dispute. Now, in return for a reported promise of $500 million in indirect U.S. aid and, according to a *60 Minutes* report, $2 billion from Saudi Arabia and Kuwait, $500 million from Japan, and $200 million from European nations, Assad agreed to assign a token force to the coalition.

Egypt's support followed, by sheer coincidence, Bush's agreement to forgive the economically troubled nation's $6.7 billion debt to the United States.

Turkey's support coincided with similar American largess. According to the Cleveland *Plain Dealer*, the United States quickly rewarded the illegal occupier of Cyprus for its opposition to Iraq's illegal occupation of Kuwait by secretly guaranteeing its fabric and clothing makers greater access to U.S. markets.

The *Plain Dealer* said the increase in import quotas for textiles—as much as 50 percent for some items—was part of a package of benefits for Turkey that also included military sales and arms transfers from U.S. and NATO allies. And though Turkey had expressed reluctance at having its bases used for any bombing missions, it suddenly reversed its position when, just days before the January 15 deadline for Iraqi withdrawal, the United States announced that it had granted Turkey $87 million in trade credits.

Even the august United Nations appeared to be open to financial rewards for its support of the Bush administration. Shortly after the U.N. Security Council approved a series of U.S. resolutions against Iraq, Secretary of State James A. Baker III asked Congress to authorize the payment of nearly $800 million in current and back dues that the United States had withheld the previous five years to protest U.N. political and management policies.

On the day the Security Council cast the crucial vote authorizing the use of force to compel Iraqi withdrawal from Kuwait, Baker showed up with a $185.7 million check payable toward the retirement of the U.S. debt.

Unsavory Allies

Of all the wheeling and dealing Bush and Baker did to forge the coalition, however, their alliances with Syria, Turkey, and Morocco struck many Mideast observers as the most hypocritical.

By their estimation, Syria's President Hafez Assad was every bit as brutal as Hussein and far more dangerous.

After all, it was Assad, not Hussein, who is suspected of organizing the 1983 terrorist attack on a U.S. compound in Lebanon that killed 241 Marines.

It was Assad, not Hussein, who apparently harbored the terrorists responsible for the destruction of Pan American Airways Flight 103 over Lockerbie, Scotland, in 1988 at a cost of 270 lives.

It was Assad, not Hussein, who was linked to a similar plot in 1987 to blow up an El Al jet carrying more than three hundred passengers from London's Heathrow Airport.

And it was Assad, not Hussein, who in 1982 ordered the destruction of the entire city of Hama and the massacre of tens of thousands of his own people who had dared to challenge his iron-fisted rule.

If the United States had had any doubts about Assad's ruthlessness, it should have learned its lesson soon after joining forces with him. According to a February 7, 1991, report in the *New York Times*, Secretary of State Baker apparently compromised the identities of two undercover agents while complaining in detail about Syrian terrorist activities during a September 14, 1990, meeting with Assad in Damascus.

Both agents were killed by Syrian terrorists a short time later, the *Times* quoted several Bush administration officials as saying.

The *Times* later reported that the agents were among a number of Jordanian intelligence operatives working inside Palestinian terrorist groups and providing Jordan with invaluable information on terrorist activities. According to the *Times*, Jordan often shared much of that data with the Central Intelligence Agency and other Western espionage services responsible for preventing terrorist acts.

American officials said they believed the terrorists obtained the information and then used it to track down informers in their ranks.

Several terrorists or terrorist groups have long been granted safe havens in Syria despite Western insistence that they be expelled. Among them are the Popular Front for the Liberation of Palestine, General Command, which Western officials believe blew up the Pan Am jet.

The *Times* said undercover penetrations of terrorist groups are among the most difficult tasks in espionage, so the loss of the agents was viewed as "especially grave."

Assad placed Syria on an aggressive course shortly after he seized power in 1970. Fearful that the civil war in Lebanon would endanger his rule, Assad sent 40,000 troops into Syria's Western neighbor in 1976 to prevent a progressive coalition from gaining power. Since then, Syrian troops have routinely persecuted forces of both the left and right, assassinated key political leaders, and participated in widespread smuggling and drug trafficking.

When Syria ousted Gen. Michel Aoun, commander of the Lebanese army's Christian faction, in October 1990 after he had refused to recognize Syria's hand-picked puppet president of Lebanon, some eight hundred Christian civilians were massacred in one day. An estimated one hundred soldiers were executed after they had surrendered to Syrian troops, and numerous other Lebanese disappeared after Assad's troops seized areas previously controlled by the Christians.

Assad then began interfering with the efforts of his longtime foe, the Palestine Liberation Organization, to provide social and economic services for the 500,000 Palestinians who live in Lebanese refugee camps.

Assad has also repeatedly massed troops on Syria's border with Jordan in an effort to keep King Hussein from pursuing pro-Palestinian policies.

The middleman in the U.S. *rapprochement* with Syria reportedly was Saudi Arabia, which has traditionally used Syria's strategic position to hamper its own enemies. Assad's takeover of Lebanon, in fact, was largely financed by the Saudis.

Critics properly contended that, by allying itself with Assad, the United States had given the man known as "The Sphinx" (after the mythical Egyptian monster that strangled passers-by who were unable to solve its riddle) a new lease on life just when he was being hampered by a loss of aid from the disintegrating communist bloc.

U.S. officials said they had few illusions about Assad, but they also viewed him as a key player in attempts to reduce Mideastern terrorism, obtain the release of Western hostages in Lebanon, provide a long-term deterrent to Iraq, and push peace between the Israelis and Arabs.

As if to validate American suspicions about his duplicity, on the eve of a March 13 postwar visit to Damascus by Secretary of State Baker, officials said Syria took delivery of twenty launchers and two dozen North Korean-made Scud missiles, possibly with chemical warheads, that could easily reach adjacent Israel.

With good reason, some feared the Bush administration would

make the same mistakes with Assad that it did with its former friend Hussein.

"They pulled up next to Saddam Hussein, called him an ally, and pretended he wasn't a bad guy," Jack G. Healey, director of Amnesty International USA, told the Associated Press. "They'll end up with exactly the same thing with Assad."

Healey charged on *60 Minutes,* and repeated to AP, that Syrian torture methods were so creative in their cruelty that Syria has become "almost a research center for torture." He said Amnesty had documented thirty-five methods of torture. Among the worst, he said, was the "Syrian chair," which snaps the spines of those strapped into it.

Despite Syria's membership in the anti-Iraq coalition, the nation remained on a list of seven countries ineligible for American aid and most trade because of its support of terrorism.

A State Department official told AP that Syria deserved credit for apparently forcing terrorists to "put a lid" on activities designed to carry out Saddam Hussein's threats of widespread violence during the six-week allied war with Iraq. But Vincent Canistraro, who until recently had been the CIA's top counterterrorism official, said, "That just proves how much control they can exert over these groups when they want."

Canistraro also noted that Syria hadn't tried to influence the Hezbollah radicals who still held thirteen Western hostages, including six Americans.

New York Times columnist William Safire also had doubts about Assad's motives and future reliability.

"Like Lucky Luciano in World War II, who won his way out of jail by ordering the Mafia not to sabotage New York harbor, Assad is winning plaudits for telling his terrorists to lay off the coalition as it brought down his longtime rival," Safire wrote.

"But peace cannot be won by demanding Israel abandon the [Golan] heights. The CIA knows that the Syrian defense minister

was in Moscow last week spending its anti-Saddam bonus from
Saudi Arabia on improved Scuds and accurate SS-21 missiles; Assad
lined up with us tactically, but he is not on peace's side."

Turkey's tyrant, President Turgut Ozal, was another who
benefited a great deal by joining the anti-Iraq coalition. Ozal's regime
was facing imminent collapse when renewed U.S. interest—and
aid—came to the rescue.

Ozal was able to support the coalition effort despite immense
opposition from his citizens, who strongly opposed warring with
another Islamic nation, because his long incumbency under rigged
elections had made him immune from public pressure.

Using the threat of war as a pretense, Ozal further emasculated
Turkey's already weak parliament and proceeded to attack any
group that opposed his decision. Some demonstrators reportedly
were shot or run over by tanks, strikes were outlawed, and the
press was censored even more than it already had been.

Ozal also stepped up his long repression of Turkey's large
Kurdish minority. Kurdish guerrillas have been fighting since 1984
to set up an independent nation, Kurdistan, where the borders
of Turkey, Iran, Iraq, and Syria converge.

On March 7, he extended emergency rule for four months
in southeast Turkey in the wake of a Kurdish rebellion against
Hussein in Iraq and protests on the Turkish side. The Interior
Ministry said the emergency rule, which permitted civilian governors
to impose curfews, ban rallies, restrict the press, and control or
prohibit union activities, would apply to ten provinces. The area
had been under martial or emergency rule almost continuously
since 1980.

Also on March 7, a semiofficial Turkish news agency reported
that a Kurdish woman had been killed and seven other Kurds
wounded the previous day when security forces broke up a protest
in the town of Idil, southeast of Ankara, the Turkish capital.

The five hundred demonstrators had been protesting the March 4 deaths of two Kurds in Idil, when police opened fire.

At the same time he was brutally suppressing the Kurds in Turkey, Ozal astonished officials of his own government and foreign observers alike by opening contacts with Iraqi Kurds fighting to overthrow Saddam Hussein.

On March 12 Ozal's government announced that it would be sending humanitarian aid to Iraqi Kurds and that it was weighing a rebel request to serve as a conduit for arms to Kurdish rebels, who claimed at that point to control large areas of northern Iraq but feared an Iraqi army counterattack.

"The Kurds are being manipulated one way or the other. Everyone else is talking to them. Why not us?" Ozal said in announcing the meeting. "These are not our enemies. We must be friends with them, as much as possible."

(One month to the day later, though, Turkey denied Iraqi allegations that it had encouraged the Kurds to rebel. "Turkey has repeatedly stated that it has no intention or design to interfere in the domestic affairs of Iraq," a Foreign Ministry spokesman said in a statement.)

By authorizing talks with the Iraqis, diplomats said, Ozal signaled Turkey's desertion of its policy of nonintervention in the affairs of its neighbors, and dropped a fifty-year-old Turkish policy of refusing to deal with Kurdish political leaders.

Foreign observers said Ozal's surprising about-face was a bald attempt to put Turkey in a positive position in the postwar era, especially in the oil-rich northern areas of Iraq.

Ozal's opponents—and even some of his supporters—warned that his initiative could greatly complicate Turkey's strained relations with its twelve million minority Kurds.

The Kurds reportedly were told that Turkey could not accept the emergence of an independent Kurdish state in what is now northern Iraq, but that it would not object to an autonomous

Kurdish region in confederation with whatever government might replace Hussein's.

"It's a big break with the past, and Ozal is flying by the seat of his pants—another one-man show," said one European diplomat. "But remember that he has very good instincts and a way of ending up on the winning side."

That was exactly what Ozal seemed to be doing in Cyprus, too, where his involvement in the anti-Iraq coalition seemed to make it even less likely that Turkey would ever be forced to comply with U.N. Security Council resolutions demanding that it withdraw its 30,000 troops.

After its 1974 invasion of the island, Turkey forced more than 200,000 Greek Cypriots to move to the south. Their property was then looted and shipped to Turkey just as Kuwaiti goods were shipped back to Iraq. Some three thousand Greek Cypriots were also sent to Turkey, where they disappeared in the nation's internationally notorious prisons.

While the rest of the world focused on what Hussein was doing in Kuwait, Ozal was planning for the settlement of the the city of Famagusta by Turkish colonists in direct defiance of Security Council Resolution 550, which was passed in 1984.

And how does the United States respond to Ozal's arrogance? With $500 million a year in military aid.

No wonder Yemen's foreign minister turned down much-needed American aid during the gulf crisis, pointing out that if the United States could help pay for the invasion and occupation of Cyprus, it could at least try to resolve the Kuwait problem through peaceful means.

But, as one Greek newspaper wisely noted by comparing the two nations' principal exports, "Apparently it's easier to overlook principles when the issue is oranges and not oil."

On March 7, Amnesty International ranked both Syria and

Turkey as being among the worst of the more than forty nations that subject women prisoners to "barbaric" treatment.

Noting that governments "often exploit a woman's family connections to break her or her relatives," the report gave special recognition to Syria, where more than seventy women have been detained during the past four years "because of the political activities of their husbands and sons." (Amnesty, which opposes capital punishment in all cases, also cited the United States for having thirty women under such sentences. But that report, unlike the one on Kuwait, didn't seem to concern President Bush.)

Another member of the American-led coalition sounded just as bad, in an Amnesty International report issued a few weeks later.

Amnesty said that more than a thousand people had been convicted in unfair trials in Morocco in the previous three months alone, including many whose confessions had been extracted through torture.

"This short circuit of justice and abuse of prisoners comes as no surprise in Morocco," the report said. "This is how the government has dealt with its opponents for more than three decades."

Like Turkey, Morocco occupies territory to which it has no legal claim. Although the World Court ruled against Morocco's seizure of the Western Sahara in 1975, the nation still maintains control over the region, despite strong-armed opposition from the indigenous Polisario Front.

Hundreds of people in the Western Sahara suspected of opposing Moroccan rule over the territory and supporting the Polisario Front had "disappeared" during the previous fifteen years, according to Amnesty's report. Hundreds of government opponents in Morocco itself also had "disappeared" in recent years.

The report said the abuses were consistent with a pattern throughout the reign of King Hassan II, who took power in 1961, the same year Amnesty was founded.

"As long as we've been going, they've been going," Amnesty spokeswoman Karen Sherlock told the Associated Press. "And still nothing's really changed in Morocco: torture, disappearances, imprisonment in horrible conditions."

Among those recently convicted were one hundred people who had joined in demonstrations against Morocco's participation in the Persian Gulf War, the report said. In one case, eight people were arrested after peacefully participating in a pro-Iraqi demonstration in January. All eight apparently were tortured and held incommunicado before trial, then transferred to a hospital by order of the prosecutor before appearing in court. The courts refused to hear allegations of torture or to allow independent medical examinations, Amnesty said. Of the eight protesters, six were given one-month sentences and two were released.

Torture is as gruesome as it is common in Morocco. "Prisoners have their heads immersed in buckets of urine, are given electric shocks, and are suspended in contorted positions in torture methods called the 'airplane' or the 'parrot,' " the report said.

The brutal track records of Syria, Turkey, and Morocco obviously seemed to be immaterial to the United States during the Persian Gulf crisis, however. All that mattered was the liberation of Kuwait and the destruction of Saddam Hussein.

Although Hussein was consistently called intransigent by the Bush administration, the record shows otherwise. Clearly, as Bush's noose began to tighten around him, Hussein began to seek a face-saving way out. But the United States wasn't about to give him one.

As early as August 12, for example, the Iraqi president announced that he was prepared to withdraw from Kuwait if Israel also withdrew from its occupied territories. The American response to this overture was to announce that the U.S. Navy would begin interdicting Iraqi oil shipments.

A week later, Hussein offered to free all foreigners in Iraq and Kuwait if the United States promised to withdraw its forces from Saudi Arabia and guarantee that the international embargo would be lifted. The offer was bluntly rejected.

Then, on October 17, U.S. and Kuwaiti officials rejected a compromise offer from Hussein under which Iraq would pull troops out of most of Kuwait, saying the pullout must be total and unconditional.

Invasion Opens Mideast Doors

It was becoming increasingly apparent to many that Bush's goals were more than the defense of Saudi Arabia, or even Iraqi withdrawal from Kuwait.

"Instead," Thomas Harrison and Joanne Landy argued in *Peace & Democracy News,* "the Iraqi invasion . . . served as an excuse for a massive assertion of U.S. power in the Middle East and an opportunity, in the words of Secretary James Baker, 'to solidify the ground rules of the new order' in the post-Cold War world.

"What is at stake for the U.S. government in the present crisis is oil and American global power, not democracy or the rights of small nations," Harrison and Landy wrote.

Dilip Hiro expanded on this theme in an article published in the British magazine *New Statesman & Society,* in which he wrote:

> When the dust of battle clears in the gulf region, a restoration of business as usual will mean more grotesque inequality, more resentment, and in time, another Saddam Hussein to voice anger of the Arab poor.
> The gulf region contains 54 percent of the world's known oil reserves. Ensuring cheap access to this energy source for

the West and Japan has formed one pillar of U.S. Middle Eastern policy since the Second World War. The others have been support for the state of Israel and hostility to Soviet influence. These aims have meant shoring up the widely despised ruling dynasties of Saudi Arabia and five smaller Persian Gulf states: Kuwait, Oman, Bahrain, Qatar and the United Arab Emirates.

Even in Kuwait, where the ruling Sabah family ran the least vicious of the regions' family businesses, the national assembly had been suspended for four years prior to the invasion. Of 1.9 million Kuwaiti residents, only 750,000 had citizenship rights, and only 60,000 males were allowed to vote.

Hiro also contended that it was Saudi Arabia, which "has never bothered with such niceties as parliaments," that had pushed Kuwait into suspending its own powerless parliament.

Yet [Fahd's] kingdom, which is now the heart of Operation Desert Storm, has courted and won American favor from the moment of its birth in 1932. Within a year, the Standard Oil Company of California cut a lucrative deal with Abdul Aziz ibn Abdul Rahman al Saud, the tribal leader who had created the nation by seizing lands from the Ottoman Turks. This broke the regional pattern that had seen all concession until then granted to British companies.

U.S. oil companies and their government have stood at the shoulder of Saudi autocrats ever since. . . . Senior Saudi princes have made hundreds of millions of dollars from kickbacks on contracts given to Western firms. The pickings are richest on weapons procurement, where the Saudis have spent on a grand scale in recent years.

Washington Post reporter Scott Armstrong first revealed where much of that money would be spent during the 1980s in a November 1, 1981, article. He reported that the Reagan administration's decision to sell airborne warning and control systems (AWACS) planes to Saudi Arabia foreshadowed a "grand defense strategy" for Mideast oil fields by constructing surrogate bases in Saudi Arabia, equipped and ready for American forces to use—which is exactly what happened in August 1990.

"The secret strategy . . . would allow the U.S. Rapid Deployment Force to move 'over the horizon' to these forward bases and pre-positioned supplies if the Soviet Union or other hostile forces attempted to capture the Persian Gulf oil fields, upon which American and other Western nations depend," Armstrong reported.

"U.S. air and naval forces, as well as the RDF [Rapid Deployment Force], also could depend upon this military infrastructure if Middle East oil is in jeopardy."

Even more prophetically, Armstrong reported that planners "envision that someday the alliance also will include Egypt, and will coordinate its military role in the region."

Armstong added that Congress was to be kept in the dark about the program by being presented parts of it in a way that would make them seem unrelated. The Saudis were also advised on how to buy much of the equipment needed directly from contractors, and to break down the orders so that the purchase amounts would be under those required to be reported to Congress.

The backbone of the defense system was to be an integrated command, control, and communications (C^3) system that would allow battlefield commanders "to calculate almost instantly the precise location of enemy ground, air and naval forces and target them with the most efficient and effective battle plan from computer display consoles in a central command post."

The deadline for completion of the program, Armstrong said, was 1990. And, judging from the performance of the coalition forces during the Persian Gulf War, that goal must have been met.

By mid-September, the CIA estimated that sanctions and the naval blockade had reduced Iraq's imports and exports by 90 percent, but the agency also predicted that the embargo would not be enough to force Hussein to withdraw from Kuwait for several more months.

By late October, Bush's patience had worn thin. Frustrated that Hussein hadn't backed down when faced with threats and bravado, Bush decided to up the ante. After discussions with Joint Chiefs of Staff Chairman Colin Powell, Secretary of Defense Dick Cheney, Secretary of State Baker, and others, Bush decided on October 31 to double the size of the U.S. force in the gulf to over 400,000 troops, in order to give the coalition "an offensive option."

Trick, No Treats

In keeping with the Halloween spirit, though, Bush treated the American people to a ghoulish trick: He kept his frightening decision from them until November 8—two days after congressional elections, because he feared it would cost his party votes.

Bush formalized his decision by dispatching three more divisions to Saudi Arabia. Two of them were the last of America's armored divisions. With no armored divisions left, the Army couldn't rotate its tank units into and out of Saudi Arabia. And since U.S. troops couldn't remain in the harsh Saudi desert indefinitely, Bush's "offensive option" was actually an offensive *imperative*.

Bush also realized that, within a matter of months, the desert's sand would begin to diminish the effectiveness of the ten-division U.S. ground force. That meant we would soon have to use it or lose it.

For some reason, Bush was surprised by the public's negative reaction to his announcement. The president's rating had already dropped by more than twenty points because of the fall budget fiasco and concern about the gulf crisis. The surveys also showed that the majority of Americans still favored giving sanctions more time to work. Only about 25 percent favored military action.

So when polls showed that Hussein's efforts to acquire nuclear weapons and his possession of chemical and biological weapons were what concerned them most about the Baghdad Bully, Bush began to hammer home on those issues as hard as he could while escalating his attacks on Hussein as being "worse than Hitler."

On November 22, the president announced that Iraq might be only months away from developing nuclear weapons. Yet Bush's own intelligence estimates said it would be more than five years before Hussein had a crude nuclear device, and ten years or more before he had a deliverable nuclear weapon.

"This message, however, did not get through right from the start, because a surfeit of untruths, half-truths and unfounded assertions about Iraq's nuclear capabilities, based on 'secret sources,' had been accumulating since the invasion," Mark D. Hibbs, European editor of McGraw-Hill's *Nucleonics Week* and *Nuclear Fuel* wrote in the Center for War, Peace and the News Media's journal *Deadline*. "Unprepared reporters who scrambled for background information immediately after Bush dropped Saddam's 'bomb' were at a disadvantage."

Hibbs blamed much of the confusion on the rabidly pro-war *New York Times* columnist William Safire, who wrote four articles contending that Iraq was on the verge of deploying nuclear weapons.

In a November 5 column, Safire claimed Iraq had twenty-six centrifuges in place, and implied that Hussein would soon have all the bombs he wanted.

Hibbs quoted Safire as writing that "with the first few thousand [centrifuges] off the line, a 'cascade can be set up . . . [and] turn out fifty pounds of weapons-grade uranium—enough for a city-destroying atom bomb—every three months.' " Hibbs continued:

Engineers at U.S. weapons labs know that the leap from
centrifuge parts, which Iraq had acquired, to working "cascades"
is at this point a pure leap of imagination. Even with twenty-
six working centrifuges—and the source for this assertion is
still unknown—Iraq would have one bomb's worth of uranium
in about eighty years. Getting the "first few thousand" centrifuges
would require a monumental manufacturing effort that U.S.
agencies do not now believe possible in Iraq. Brazil, whose
military has sought the bomb since 1975, has the required
infrastructure. But after throwing hundreds of millions of dollars
into centrifuge development for fifteen years, Brazil has a few
hundred crude machines that grind out enriched uranium so
slowly that the country is probably a few years away from a
single bomb's worth.

Moreover, there is a hitch in linking centrifuges into the
"cascades" needed to get bomb-grade product. As you add more
and more machines, the problem of keeping the "cascade" airtight
mounts. If you do not get everything just right, your centrifuges
explode or "crash."

Unfortunately, Hibbs said, *60 Minutes* contributed contradictory but equally frightening misinformation when it reported
that Hussein's efforts had been slowed "because he lacked the
necessary raw material"—but the Iraqis had overcome this problem,
he said, by mining a plentiful amount of uranium "right on [its]
own doorstep."

Actually, Hibbs said, Iraq already had plenty of uranium. It
just lacked the ability to do anything with it, Safire's allegations
to the contrary.

"Right now," Hibbs wrote, "credible estimates of the amount
of time Hussein needs, even under optimal conditions, to make
bomb-grade uranium and use it in a nuclear weapon are still
measured in years, not months; that is, just about where they were
on August 2, when the Iraqi dictator invaded Kuwait."

Regardless, thanks largely to the boost in support he got by dropping Hussein's mythical 'bomb' on the American public, Bush was soon able to make sure that those "optimal conditions" for Iraq were once again far into the future.

The by-then-obsessed Bush also made sure the nation's chemical-weapons capabilities were crippled, if not destroyed—although those capabilities, too, may have been greatly exaggerated.

In fact, even the most universally accepted belief—first articulated by then-Secretary of State George Shultz—that Hussein had used chemical weapons on Kurds in 1988 has been challenged by a study published by none other than the U.S. Army War College.

In *Iraqi Power and U.S. Security in the Middle East*, researchers Stephen C. Pelletiere, Douglas V. Johnson II, and Leif R. Rosenberger conclude that the highly publicized gassing of the Kurds was more likely the work of Iran than of Iraq. They note that survivors testified that the chemical weapons were dropped from planes well after the town had been captured by Iranian forces and after fighting in the area had ended. What's more, they note, the Iranians went to suspicious lengths to make the atrocity public, taking the unusual step of inviting the international press and human-rights organizations to see the bodies and interview the survivors.

Pelletiere et al. added that, based on a review of Iraqi communications intercepted at that time, "we find it impossible to confirm the State Department's claim that [Iraqi] gas was used in this instance."

Newsday reporter Knut Royce said a congressional Mideast specialist who had also reviewed the communications intercepts agreed with the Army War College study's conclusion. "George Shultz was going . . . way beyond the evidence," the specialist told Royce.

Adding credence to that argument is that Iraq apparently

never introduced chemical agents into the combat theater, let alone tried to use them, during the Persian Gulf War.

After routing the Iraqi army, several hundred thousand allied troops combed through bunkers, storage depots, and other facilities without finding a trace of nerve gas or other chemical weapons.

"It's a great mystery," said Brig. Gen. Steven Arnold, senior operations officer for Army forces deployed in Operation Desert Storm.

Another senior officer said U.S. intelligence analysts had concluded that any chemical weapons Iraq might have had "never got distributed down to the battlefield" from storage sites north of the Euphrates River.

Washington Post staff writer Molly Moore reported from Al Jubayl, Saudi Arabia, that top Marine officers said they had found no indication of chemical weapons stockpiles on the battlefields of Kuwait.

Military commanders there described the absence of chemical weapons as one of the biggest mysteries of the conflict.

U.S. intelligence sources also concluded that reports by Kuwaiti resistance fighters that Iraqi forces were using Kuwaiti mosques and schools as chemical depots were false. Other reports, including one of a soldier being blistered with mustard gas, all proved false.

Before the war started, virtually the entire population of the gulf states was provided with gas masks due to the widespread belief that Hussein would use his Scud missiles to deliver chemical warheads.

But none of the scores of Scuds fired at Israel and Saudi Arabia carried chemical warheads. This led many analysts to conclude that Iraq does not have the capability to employ chemical warheads on the missiles.

When the ground war started, and no gas attack ensued, coalition officials at first speculated that it must have been because their units had maneuvered too quickly to be targeted. But it later appeared the Iraqis had had no intention of using such weapons, if they even had them in any numbers at all.

Hussein had warned repeatedly in the months leading up to the war that Iraq had developed binary weapons, which contain two relatively inert compounds that when mixed together during the flight of an artillery shell or bomb form a highly lethal concoction. But this may very well have been another case of Hussein's bluffing.

By November 16, the Bush administration was clearly in the coalition driver's seat. It rejected Soviet envoy Yevgeny Primakov's suggestion that a solution to the Persian Gulf crisis be linked to the problem of Israel's occupation of land claimed by Palestinians.

Two days later, Iraq announced it would free the estimated 2,000 remaining Westerners held hostage in Iraq and occupied Kuwait between Christmas and March 25, "unless something would take place that mars the atmosphere of peace." But the overture didn't change Bush's policy of "no negotiations."

On November 30, the day after the Security Council voted to authorize the use of force if Iraq didn't withdraw from Kuwait by January 15, Bush bowed to public pressure and announced he was dispatching Secretary of State Baker to Baghdad to discuss a way to end the crisis.

Though this would appear to be Bush's first and only conciliatory gesture during the entire crisis, he made it clear that the matter would be resolved his way or no way. "There will be no negotiations," he said over and over again.

On December 3, Hussein said he expected talks with the United States to include discussions of the Israeli occupation of the West Bank and Gaza Strip.

The following day, in what appeared to be another placatory move, Baghdad said it would allow all three thousand Soviets stranded in Iraq to leave, but demanded that the Kremlin pay compensation for canceling their work contracts.

On December 6, in yet another concession, Hussein urged his National Assembly to release all foreigners held as hostages by the Iraqi government.

The next day, the Iraqi parliament overwhelmingly approved Hussein's recommendation (not that it had any choice) and endorsed its leader's decision to free Western hostages. U.S. officials had nary a kind word in response.

On December 10, the first wave of American hostages freed under Hussein's release program headed home.

Then, on December 18, European leaders put on hold what could have been a crucial meeting with Iraqi diplomats after scheduled talks in Washington between Bush and Iraqi Foreign Minister Tariq Aziz were canceled as the two nations fenced over when Baker would meet with Hussein in Baghdad. Bush wanted the meeting sooner and Hussein wanted it later—on the eve of the U.N. deadline, in fact.

On December 19, Lt. Gen. Calvin Waller, deputy commander of U.S. forces in the Persian Gulf, created a minor uproar when he said U.S. troops would not be ready to mount an offensive by the January 15 deadline. On the following day, however, the Pentagon warned Hussein that U.S. air power *would* be ready to attack by January 15 even if all ground forces wouldn't be ready by then.

On Christmas Eve, Hussein was being quoted by Spanish television as saying the Israeli capital of Tel Aviv would be Iraq's first target if war broke out. After urgent consultations, he dispatched his envoys back to their posts to pass the word that he was ready to talk. Bush, meanwhile, was busy passing the word that coalition forces were ready to fight.

On January 3, though, Bush responded to Hussein's diplomatic overtures by offering to send Baker to Geneva, Switzerland, to meet Aziz in "one last attempt" at peace. Perhaps not surprisingly, the January talks turned out to be futile after Hussein again ruled out an unconditional withdrawal from Kuwait and Baker repeated that "we will not agree to anything that would constitute linkage."

On January 12, in a historic vote after three days of impassioned debate, Congress gave Bush the authority to wage war in the gulf. The White House–backed resolution passed by a comfortable 250-183 margin in the House and by a tighter, 52-47, tally in the Senate.

At that point, U.N. Secretary-General Javier Perez de Cuellar announced that he would go to Baghdad for one last try at persuading Hussein to pull out of Kuwait.

According to a transcript of the January 13 meeting later published in *Al Dustur,* a Jordanian newspaper, Hussein told Perez de Cuellar that "to utter the word 'withdrawal' [from Kuwait] while there is still a chance for war" would amount to an "enemy victory over us."

In the published transcript, Hussein said the Iraqi people "know that if the fighting erupts, they will have to pay dear sacrifices not because their adversaries are more courageous . . . but because they have weapons more sophisticated than our weapons."

Hussein also stressed that he would consider only a "full package," in which Iraqi withdrawal from Kuwait was linked to the resolution of the Palestinian problem. "Partial discussion of issues without comprehensive linkage among them will pro-duce . . . a loser and a winner, and we do not believe that this serves the cause of peace," Hussein was quoted as saying.

During the lengthy session, Perez de Cuellar noted Bush's desire to tackle the Palestinian problem, and complimented the Iraqi leader for attempts to address that issue. "Even Mr. Bush, when I saw him . . . admitted the urgent need for tackling the crisis of Pales-tine," Perez de Cuellar was reported to have said.

Afterward, Perez de Cuellar said "God only knows" if there would be war. But the rest of the world seemed to have a pretty good idea that war was inevitable.

The next day, Perez de Cuellar said he had lost hope for

peace, and Iraqi lawmakers pledged to support Hussein with their blood. At the last minute, France outlined a peace plan that called for Iraq's withdrawal from Kuwait and the convening of a general Mideast peace conference.

On January 15, the day the U.N. deadline was to expire, the U.S. State Department rejected the French plan because it linked the Kuwait and Palestinan issues.

As the clock kept ticking, tens of thousands of Americans demonstrated in Washington, New York, San Francisco, Los Angeles, and smaller towns throughout the United States, hoping to persuade Bush to give diplomacy more time.

But Bush had made up his mind. Baghdad was about to see his latest interpretation of "a thousand points of light," courtesy of a "kinder, gentler" America.

The Mother of All Battles

At 1:40 A.M. on January 17, 1991, the deep darkness of a moonless night in the Persian Gulf was pierced by the sharp crack and the sudden spark of a Tomahawk cruise missile fired from the *USS Wisconsin.*

"There it goes. Happy trails!" a voice on the deck radio of a nearby ship shouted.

Less than nineteen hours after a U.N.-mandated deadline for Iraq to withdraw from Kuwait, the Persian Gulf War had begun.

In many respects, it was to be a war unlike any other. It would feature malevolent microwaves, lethal laser beams, sinister smart bombs, furtive Stealth fighter-bombers, and camera-equipped planes that broadcast photos of missiles entering into a military complex through an open door.

In other respects, however, it was to be a war just like any other. It would feature death and destruction; the anguished cries of survivors and the last gasps of victims; blood, bones, and bodies flying through the air; and bridges, buildings, and battlements crashing to the ground.

Before it was over a frightful forty-two days later, it would also feature the largest helicopter assault in military history, the largest tank battle and armored attacks since World War II, and more than a hundred-thousand sorties (about four times the number flown against Japan during the last fourteen months of World War II).

Shortly after the first of the more than three hundred Tomahawks, at a cost of $1 million each, took flight, allied warplanes streaked north from Saudi Arabia. About ninety minutes later, the skies over Baghdad exploded with anti-aircraft fire and bursting bombs as President Bush and millions of other Americans watched on televisions in the comfort of their homes several thousand miles away.

"Let me describe for you what I see out the window now," a nervous but low-keyed CNN correspondent reported from Baghdad's Al-Rashid Hotel. "More tracer fire from the anti-aircraft guns. Another entire section of Baghdad went dark for about, oh, two seconds just now. And then the lights came back on. . . . And we continue to see the tracer fire. And off in the distance we can continue to hear . . . what may be the sound of bombs coming down."

The mood below was less sanguine, as people desperately tried to find shelter. Many didn't make it.

According to reports from the city that first night, deafening, staccato blasts shot orange plumes into the sky. They were followed by the pop-pop-pop of anti-aircraft fire that produced red, white, and green tracers. The lights went out. The air-raid sirens wailed.

A short time after the first bombs hit Baghdad, White House press secretary Marlin Fitzwater announced, in President Bush's words, "The liberation of Kuwait has begun."

Less than two hours later, in a 9 P.M. televised address, Bush described the marshaling of American and allied forces into Operation Desert Storm, and declared: "We will not fail."

Hussein, however, sounded like he was ready for the challenge. "The great war, the mother of all battles, has begun," he declared on Baghdad Radio.

But the sheer size, coordination, and ferocity of the air assault made Bush's success a safe bet. With the help of sophisticated electronic jamming devices to confuse or block Iraqi radar, and night-vision devices to pinpoint targets while shrouded in the darkness, American pilots "serviced" their targets with relative impunity.

Only four American aircraft were reported lost in the first forty-eight hours of bombing. The Pentagon said eleven of an estimated seven hundred Iraqi warplanes were destroyed.

The unending stream of laser-guided bombs and missiles destroyed power plants, oil refineries, factories, military bases, and storage depots.

"Things are going well," Bush said before dawn of the second day as the huge allied air armada continued pounding away at Iraq.

American investors seemed to agree. Crude oil prices took their deepest one-day plunge in history, while New York's stock market soared to its second-largest point gain in history. Nothing like a good little war to help the economy.

The accuracy of the the allies' "smart bombs" diminished quickly, however. So did that of the touted Tomahawk missiles, which began hitting the wrong targets because their pre-programmed digital maps became outdated after landmark buildings were destroyed. As a result, what the military briefers called "collateral damage" soon began to include museums, shops, office buildings, homes— and people.

Upping the Ante

Then Hussein struck back. On the second evening of the war, Iraq attacked Israel with at least eight Scud missiles. None were armed with the much-feared chemical warheads, and only about a dozen people were injured. But the Baghdad Bully had clearly upped the ante.

The allies' biggest fear all along had been that Israel would retaliate and shatter the Arab-Western coalition. In telephone conversations with officials in Washington, Israeli Defense Minister Moshe Arens reportedly expressed the Israeli military's desire to strike back, as it had in past conflicts. But the American officials apparently reminded Arens that Israel hadn't been given the codes that help pilots to distinguish friend from foe.

Without such codes, Israeli planes would be entering the war zone at great risk. American officials feared Israel would send them anyway, but after three hours of intense negotiations, Israel agreed to delay—but not rule out—a response.

In return for its cooperation, the United States rushed a shipment of U.S.-manned Patriot defensive missile batteries, with their enhanced radar-tracking devices, to Israel. The Patriot already had proved to be highly effective against the inaccurate "Scud duds" fired on Saudi Arabia.

Or so we were told: "Forty-two Scuds engaged, forty-one intercepted," Bush later bragged when he visited a crowd of cheering workers on February 15 at the factory where the Patriot is built. What the president *didn't* tell his proud audience was that it took one hundred and twenty Patriots to intercept those forty-one Scuds.

But the effectiveness issue went beyond the fact that it took three or sometimes four Patriots to down one Scud.

"When I go back and look at the individual shots to figure out which ones they are counting as hits and misses, I come up with several that might have been misses. And even when you did hit, you still have several tons of metal coming down," John Pike, a weapons expert with the Federation of American Scientists, told *Chicago Tribune* military affairs writer David Evans.

ABC-TV correspondent Leslie Cockburn watched four Patriots that were launched over Tel Aviv one night. Evans quoted her as saying, "The first self-destructed. The second and third roared across town *below* the level of high-rise office buildings and then hit in Tel Aviv. The fourth one flew up, did a wonderful hairpin maneuver and came down and exploded next to a restaurant called Mandy's. The citizens were just as at risk from falling Patriots as they were from Scuds."

Another problem with Patriots was brought to light in March by columnist William Safire, who apparently had found new and better sources after the war than those he had quoted in his strongly disputed columns on Iraq's nuclear threat before the war.

According to Safire, "The interceptions—those great midair explosions that thrilled us all—did not, in many and perhaps most cases, stop the Scuds from delivering their payload of high explosives."

So what did the Patriots hit?

"Fuel tanks," wrote Safire. "Most Scuds began to break up on re-entry in the atmosphere, about 15 to 12 kilometers in the air; this has been derogated as poor Iraqi adaption of the Soviet-built missile, but at that dropping stage the warhead no longer needs the fuel tank; the explosive payload is well on its way to the general target area."

Because of their great inaccuracy, however, the Scuds rarely scored direct hits on significant targets during most of the war. When one of them finally—and tragically—did, in the war's final days, it cost twenty-eight Americans their lives.

But since public perception—although based on deception—was that the Patriot had been a great success, politicians and generals immediately began using that belief not only to push development of the obscenely expensive Strategic Defense Initiative, but also of a $40 billion system called G-Pals, an acronym for "global protection against limited strikes."

While the Scuds continued to rain terror on Israel and Saudi Arabia, the Iraqi Air Force was a virtual no-show. The allies waited and waited for a counterattack that never came.

Sunday, January 20, proved to be a trying day for the allies, as Iraqi television showed two blindfolded POWs being paraded through the streets of Baghdad, and later broadcast interviews with several apparently brutalized downed pilots, some of whom said later that most of their injuries actually had been caused by ejecting from their jets. At least one said he had also self-inflicted additional injuries in the vain hope that his appearance would keep him from being forced to say things on television.

At any rate, the number of POWs mounted on January 20, when a total of fifteen allied planes, nine of them American, were reported lost.

On Tuesday, January 22, an Iraqi Scud missile eluded the Patriot anti-missile defense system in Israel once again, and hit Tel Aviv. It killed one person, caused two to die of heart attacks, and injured about a hundred others.

Oil prices suddenly jumped sharply, and the stock market retreated. Nothing like a bad little war to hurt the economy.

But, as the war entered its second week, Gen. Colin Powell put a positive spin on its status. After twelve thousand sorties, he said, allied forces had achieved "air superiority" and now intended to concentrate on the Iraqi ground forces in and around Kuwait.

Hussein tried to prove Powell wrong the following day, but ended up proving him right. The Iraqi air force finally came out of hiding to conduct its first combat attack. In a one-sided battle, though, a Saudi pilot shot down two Iraqi jets carrying Exocet missiles that were probably intended for allied ships thousands of feet below in the Persian Gulf.

"Clean" War Gets Dirty

On Friday, January 25, the world learned that the up-till-then sanitary war was dirty business after all. But that didn't mean television viewers finally saw the blood and guts that make up any war. Instead, they saw photos of what military officials said was a world-record oil spill allegedly caused when Iraq sabotaged Kuwait's main supertanker loading pier to hamper amphibious landings and shut down Saudi desalting plants, which provide most of the country's fresh water.

The next day, U.S. F-111s fired smart bombs at Kuwaiti oil facilities to stop the Iraqis from pumping more crude oil into the gulf. That was the good news. The bad news was that the slick was reported to be drifting toward the Saudi desalting plants. (As it turned out, an amphibious landing had never been planned, and the oil never seriously threatened the plants.)

Then "Khafji" entered the world's vocabulary. On January 30, in a deserted port city (not a village, as U.S. briefers kept calling it) bearing that name, the first major ground battle of the war was fought. It was there that eleven Marines became the first American ground forces to die in battle in the gulf.

Allied troops retook the town the next day, but two soldiers who were not directly involved in the fighting were reported missing. One was Army Specialist Melissa Rathbun-Nealy, who became the first and only woman soldier reported missing in action during the war. She was released unharmed after the war.

The Khafji confrontation also provided an excellent example of the Bush administration's attempts to put a positive "spin" on bad news by switching focus. Rather than having the usual staff officer brief the press that day, the job was assigned to the affable, authoritative Gen. H. Norman Schwarzkopf.

The allied commander began by showing some of the most spectacular smart-bomb videotapes reporters and television viewers had seen yet. Included was tape of a truck driver Schwarzkopf called "the luckiest man in Iraq" because he drove across a bridge seconds before the span was destroyed by a bomb. Both the general and reporters got a good laugh out of the footage.

Schwarzkopf also discussed Iraqi losses of the past day, which he described as "rather sensational." It was only then—more than twenty minutes into the briefing—that Schwarzkopf mentioned, almost in passing, that twelve Marines were "KIA" at Khafji.

KIA? Killed in Action, of course. But for most TV viewers back in America, the acronym probably took a while to sink in—which was exactly the idea.

Schwarzkopf's performance—and that's what it was—wasn't as "off the cuff" as he made it seem. According to *Newsweek,* "The general's diversionary tactic had been carefully orchestrated. On that morning, like every morning since the war began, White House, Pentagon, State Department, and CIA officials had gathered before dawn to plot the 'spin' for the day. Administration officials understand that the United States is engaged in a PR war as well as a real one."

On February 4, Iranian President Hashemi Rafsanjani made a surprise offer to mediate talks to end the war. The allies' response came in the form of more bombs on beleaguered Baghdad, reportedly blasting communications centers, government offices, and industrial installations.

The allies pounded their no-compromise message home when their aircraft bombed Hussein's hometown of Tikrit. In response, Radio Baghdad, a.k.a. Mother of Battles Radio, issued what appeared to be a terrorist call to arms with coded instructions to agents abroad. If it was, the call went unanswered. Terrorist activity continued to be almost nonexistent, thanks, it was later reported, to terrorism's biggest booster, the new "friend" of the United States, Syrian President Hafez Assad, who had put a hold on one of his favorite activities.

Meanwhile, allied bombers continued to drop tons of explosives on Iraq's elite Republican Guards along the Iraq-Kuwait border.

On February 8, coalition bombers destroyed a major communications center in Baghdad and a key bridge across the Tigris River.

In Washington, President Bush blasted Jordan's King Hussein for moving "way over into Saddam Hussein's camp," and said that some $55 million in aid earmarked for Jordan was being reviewed. Bush was responding to the king's strongly worded attack on the U.S.-led coalition's destruction of Iraq and the killing of innocent civilians when its mandate was supposed to be to drive Iraqi troops from Kuwait.

It was during this time that Iraqi aircraft mysteriously began taking refuge at Iranian airfields. Their quick flights into the neutral nation were made from airfields near the Iranian border before they could be intercepted by coalition fighter-jets. At the time of Cheney and Powell's visit, U.S. officials said the great escape had grown so much that more than eighty fighter-bombers were at the airports of Baghdad's recent enemy. To allay any suspicions of collusion, Iran said it would impound the planes until the war ended. To make sure Iran kept its word, the United States vowed to shoot down any Iraqi plane that tried to rejoin the war after taking refuge.

On February 9, Dick Cheney and Colin Powell talked for eight hours with Schwarzkopf and other U.S. military leaders about when and where to launch a ground offensive.

Cheney conceded the following day that air attacks alone probably wouldn't force Iraq out of Kuwait. But he said final approval for a ground war would be "a presidential decision."

Upon returning to Washington, Cheney and Powell met with Bush. Afterward, the president said the air war "will continue for a while."

Asked when the much-feared ground offensive might start, Bush replied. "We're not talking about dates."

Bush met with the defense chiefs of Britain and France the following day. Britain's defense minister said there was still "work to be done" in air attacks to weaken Iraqi forces before the allies launched a full-scale ground attack.

But people began to wonder why Baghdad was still undergoing such relentless bombing. The war's stated aim, after all, was to rid Kuwait of Iraqi troops, not to destroy the cradle of civilization. Bomb-weary Baghdad, said those who managed to flee to Jordan, was becoming little more than a big urban sewer. Human waste and garbage rotted in the streets because the city of 4 million people did not have power. Running water hadn't been available for weeks. Not only did that preclude showers and baths, but toilets didn't work, so gastritis and other digestive diseases began to spread rapidly. Some charged that this was as much an example of biological warfare as firing biological weapons into the city.

"Collateral Damage" Gains a Human Face

Then came the Bush administration's first potential defeat in its marvelously managed public-relations war.

Just after 4 A.M. on February 13, allied warplanes dropped two laser-guided bombs on an underground shelter in suburban Baghdad. One bomb blasted the entrance shut, trapping hundreds of men, women, and children inside. The other pierced the camouflaged roof and turned the building into an incineration chamber. Angry officials said five hundred civilians were killed, and the charred bodies shown on the world's television screens offered graphic evidence that they were probably telling the truth.

"My God! My God! All of them are dead. Why? Why? Why are you killing all the Iraqi children?" cried a man whose family of twelve had been burned beyond recognition.

"Bush, Bush, you will pay for all crimes shedding innocent blood every day," other mourners shouted as flag-draped coffins were lowered into a mass grave.

According to Western reporters on the scene, a sign lying on the ground identified the bunker as a civilian shelter, though allied commanders claimed it was a military command-and-control center. For the first time during the war, journalists were allowed to go anywhere they wanted without a censor by their side. They took advantage of the freedom to comb the facility from top to bottom. Few, if any, who did believed Bush's image-makers, who blamed Hussein for the deaths by suggesting he allowed civilians to use the structure in hopes of shielding a military bunker.

But there was a difference in American officials' approach: Many were willing to speak only on condition of anonymity.

"We know who built it, when and what for, when it was modified," one unnamed official was widely quoted as saying.

In Washington, another official anonymously confirmed that Baghdad's Al-Rashid Hotel, home to foreign reporters and diplomats, contained a key Iraqi military communications center. But he said no strike on the hotel was planned precisely because the building contained civilians. He failed to point out an important difference in the kind of civilians, however. The hotel was filled with *foreign* civilians, while the bombed shelter had been filled with *Iraqi* civilians.

One of the few officials willing to talk on the record was Navy Captain Ronald Wildermuth, the U.S. Central Command's director of public affairs. And Wildermuth didn't mince words. "This guy [Hussein] is such a slime that I would not doubt he'd put people in there," he said.

But the spin began to lose control when a London newspaper reported that U.S. commanders bombed the bunker because they believed it was sheltering key Iraqi military and civilian officials and their families, not a command-and-control center as they had claimed.

The *Independent*, a respected daily, said it based its report on comments made by a senior U.S. military official in Saudi Arabia, who spoke on condition of anonymity.

"There's not a soul who believes that it was a command-and-

control bunker," the *Independent* quoted the official as saying.
"We thought it was a military personnel bunker.

"The raid was a serious error that has caused deep distress
to America's Saudi military allies," the source continued. "We could,
by genuinely expressing our sorrow, do something to repair this."

Harish Chandola, a correspondent for *Indian Express,* one
of India's largest national newspapers, reported that he had visited
the shelter just before the war started and found it to be "a vast
concrete cavern, capable of housing the population of a small town,
with electricity, running water and toilets." He said he was told
the bunker was one of "seven or eight massive, solid shelters built
during the war with Iran."

The *Independent* maintained that the Baghdad bunker bombing came at the height of a dispute among senior Air Force officers
about the efficacy of the continued bombing of Baghdad.

In some areas, at least, the bombing was definitely backfiring.

In Jordan, which has a large Palestinian population, King
Hussein, despite Bush's threat that his outspokenness might cost
him U.S. aid, expressed outrage at the bombing. He also called
for an immediate cease-fire and an investigation by the U.N. Security
Council, as hundreds of his citizens stood outside the U.S. Embassy
in Amman chanting "Death to America!" and waving black flags
of mourning. Palestinians in a half-dozen towns and cities on the
adjacent occupied West Bank, meanwhile, started a three-day strike
to protest the deaths.

In the United States, on the other hand, there was little indication that the incident had changed many views.

"My opinion stayed the same," Reggie Rejniak, a 36-year-
old carriage driver in Philadelphia told the *New York Times.* "I'm
sure it was an accidental bombing. I don't think our government
is into civilian bombings. Accidents happen in war. You can't avoid
them."

Gorbachev Pushes Peace

At the same time, Soviet President Mikhail S. Gorbachev stepped up his peace-making efforts by meeting with Kuwait's foreign minister. "The time is such that we have something to discuss," he told reporters.

Gorbachev dispatched Yevgeny M. Primakov, his personal adviser and an old hand at Mideast diplomacy, to Baghdad. At the war's conclusion, Primakov published part of his account in the Communist newspaper *Pravda,* for which he was a foreign correspondent in the 1960s.

Primakov arrived at the Al-Rashid Hotel in downtown Baghdad late the night of February 11 after traveling from the Iranian border in a speeding cavalcade of camouflaged cars.

The hotel had no electricity or running water, but Primakov said conditions were still better there that at the Soviet Embassy, whose thirteen staff members were living in what they hoped were bomb-proof seven-foot-wide steel tubes buried in the embassy garden.

The morning after his arrival, Primakov first met with Foreign Minister Tarik Aziz, who made wild accusations about Soviet collusion with the United States to destroy Iraq.

"I told Aziz that Iraq was making one mistake after another by trying to preserve what was beyond preservation and driving itself deeper into a dead-end," Primakov wrote. "When the stream of abuse continued, I said we had not come to listen to this kind of talk. If it would be the same from Saddam Hussein, perhaps I should not waste my time."

Aziz calmed down at that point, and a short time later escorted Primakov to a meeting with Hussein at a government guest house. When Hussein took off his coat and unbuckled his gun belt, Primakov said, he was surprised to see that the Iraqi dictator had lost a substantial amount of weight since October, when they had last met.

Primakov said that he told Hussein that "the Americans absolutely favor a broad-scale land operation as a result of which the Iraqi task force in Kuwait will be completely destroyed. Do you understand—destroyed?"

Primakov then detailed Gorbachev's proposal: the announcement of a complete and unconditional Iraqi withdrawal from Kuwait as quickly as possible.

"Here, for the first time, I saw change," Primakov wrote. "Saddam Hussein started to ask questions—how could he be sure his soldiers would not be shot in the back as they withdrew? Would air strikes at Iraq be stopped after the troops left? Would sanctions be lifted?"

But Hussein was still noncommital. He suggested sending Aziz to Moscow for more talks.

"There is no time left—you must act immediately," Primakov replied. Hussein finally began earnestly discussing how to resolve the crisis.

In the Mideast tradition, however, the haggling went on for several more days. Aziz shuttled between Baghdad and Moscow, giving a little more ground each time.

On the same day as the bunker bombing, meanwhile, the U.N. Security Council had held its first private formal session in sixteen years; the United States had said an open meeting might cause Hussein to think the coalition was divided.

Britain took it on the PR chin the same day, when a second human-rights group, Middle East Watch, accused it of violating the Geneva Conventions and international law by rounding up and imprisoning Iraqis and Palestinians living in Britain.

In a special bulletin, the group charged that many of the prisoners should not have been held at all, that thirty-five who were being held as prisoners of war legally should have been considered civilian detainees, and that judicial proceedings for all of them failed to meet the standards of international law.

"The roundup of scores of Arabs residing in Britain did not begin with the outbreak of hostilities on the morning of January 17," the report said. "Since Iraq invaded Kuwait on August 2, the Home Office has issued notices of intention-to-deport to a total of one-hundred-sixty-seven Iraqis, Palestinians, Lebanese, and Yemenis. Immigration rules since January 17 bar all Iraqi nationals from entering the country and all those already in the U.K. from renewing their residency permits."

The group also noted that the Geneva Conventions forbid holding civilian internees in prison, but that all the Arabs under detention in Britain were in one prison or another.

In Washington, meanwhile, a group of liberal lawmakers said Bush should set aside any plans to intensify the war by beginning a ground offensive.

"It is our belief that there is no need to escalate the war in the Persian Gulf," said the one-sentence statement signed by forty-one Democratic members of Congress and one independent.

Thus the bombing occurred just as an increasing number of questions about the scope of the war were being raised.

The prior week, U.N. Secretary-General Javier Perez de Cuellar criticized as "inadmissible" the allied bombing of Jordanian trucks on the road from Baghdad to Amman, and repeated his discomfort with the death and suffering of civilians after the shelter bombing.

Gorbachev, meanwhile, had said the air war was assuming "an ever more alarming and dramatic scope," and that the "logic" of allied military actions threatened to exceed the U.N. mandate.

Even Senate GOP Leader Bob Dole of Kansas conceded that there was a "bit of truth to what Gorbachev says." Dole added that Bush's war objectives seemed to have gone beyond the four goals originally set: freeing Kuwait, restoring its government, stabilizing the region, and safeguarding Americans there.

"I think an implicit objective now is to destroy Iraq militarily, and, if you can, destroy Saddam Hussein," Dole said. "That wasn't one of the four objectives . . . but it's sort of taken on a life of its own."

At the United Nations, meanwhile, Algeria, India, and several other nonaligned nations began pushing for a debate on whether the war was exceeding the U.N. mandate.

The U.N. mandate consisted of twelve Security Council resolutions passed between August and December. The broadest was Resolution 678, which set the January 15 deadline for Iraqi withdrawal from Kuwait and said the allies could use "all necessary means" to uphold the resolutions "and to restore international peace and security in the region."

But some international legal experts had been critical of the resolutions from the beginning. Burns H. Weston, a law professor at the University of Iowa, told a conference of the American Bar Association that Resolution 678 gave the "appearance of the U.N. having been used as a tool of U.S. foreign policy . . . and raised questions about the extent to which the U.N. has been allowed to keep faith with its own charter."

Weston claimed many delegates who voted for Resolution 678 saw it as authorizing force only as a last resort.

Nubar Housepian, a political science professor at Hunter College, agreed. He was quoted as saying that the implicit U.S. goal of removing Hussein is "clearly a violation of the U.N. resolution."

Housepian also maintained that the bombing had cut off drinking water to Baghdad in violation of Article 54 of Protocol 1 of the Geneva Convention, which says that, "in no event shall actions . . . be taken which may be expected to leave the civilian population with such inadequate food or water as to cause its starvation."

Sensing that momentum was swinging his way, Hussein offered to comply with the U.N. resolution demanding Iraq's unconditional withdrawal from Kuwait, and called for an immediate cease-fire. But Hussein said the withdrawal must be coupled with the pullout from the region of allied forces and should be simultaneous with an Israeli withdrawal from the occupied lands; thus Bush called Hussein's offer a "cruel hoax," and the bombing continued.

Hussein's provocative prose probably didn't help his case.

"The United States and members of the unholy alliance sent their planes, which fire rockets from far away, and their long-range missiles to drop enormous amounts of bombs and explosives on women, children, and old people in all Iraqi cities and villages, even the nomadic Bedouin in the desert," his statement read.

"Their latest crime was the ugly and dirty crime of intentionally bombing a civilian shelter that killed and burned hundreds of women, children, and old people.

"The United States and its allies launched a dirty and cowardly war against a proud and brave people. Iraq triumphed in this confrontation. It triumphed because it remained solid, courageous, faithful, dignified, and strong-willed. It triumphed because it upheld the spiritual principles and values emanating from its true religion and rich heritage."

Despite Hussein's exaggerated rhetoric, the United Nations' Perez de Cuellar said the offer deserved "careful study."

On Monday, February 18, Iraqi Foreign Minister Tariq Aziz met for three and a half hours with Gorbachev in Moscow, in an effort to avoid a full-scale ground war.

"Now, time is the crucial factor," Primakov, in his *Pravda* article, quoted Gorbachev as saying. "If you value the lives of your countrymen and the fate of Iraq, you must act immediately."

Through long, slow, and "excruciatingly difficult" talks, Aziz inched toward meeting the U.N. resolutions.

Finally, Gorbachev got Iraq's agreement to a plan he thought would at least give the negotiators some breathing room. But when Gorbachev called coalition leaders, Primakov said he discovered that "a significant shift" had occurred in their attitudes between Iraq and the coalition.

The remaining differences, Primakov wrote, "were insignificant and amenable to agreement at the U.N. Security Council within one or two days."

Gorbachev sent Aziz back to Baghdad with a new peace proposal that the Soviets said included a call for an "unconditional withdrawal from Kuwait."

At the United Nations, the Soviet U.N. ambassador told the Security Council that Moscow's plan sought the rapid pullout of Iraq from Kuwait and negotiations to resolve differences on the other U.N. resolutions.

But Bush unilaterally rejected the proposal, saying there could be no negotiations and no concessions. No one seemed to want to remind the petulant president that the coalition was supposedly a U.N. operation and that Bush had never been formally named to lead it.

On February 21, Iraq and the Soviet Union agreed on steps that could lead to an Iraqi withdrawal and an end to the war. Although Bush had "serious concerns about several points" in the plan, White House spokesman Marlin Fitzwater said the president would study it closely.

While he did, Baghdad Radio railed at the allies' "bestial crimes," but also expressed Iraq's "honest desire to establish security and stability in the region."

Hussein had sent similar mixed messages in a speech the day before. After defiantly declaring that Iraq was "ready for the showdown," he also said he wanted peace.

But Bush no longer did. Sen. Richard Lugar of Indiana, one of Bush's top Republican mouthpieces, said on NBC's *Today* show that the Soviet-sponsored talks were "not in our best interest at all."

"We are attempting, I suppose, to retain some good humor with Mikhail Gorbachev. But the plans which have come forward this week are almost as difficult to fathom as the ones last Friday," Lugar said. "Clearly we ought to continue to prosecute the war.

We ought to continue to push Iraq out of Kuwait unconditionally."

Rep. Lee Hamilton, interviewed on the same program, said the Soviets' proposed peace plan had "very positive aspects." But he added that it also had "plenty of things wrong with it," primarily the lifting of sanctions on Iraq.

"The problem here is that we are poised on the brink, I think, of a decisive military victory," the Indiana Democrat said. "You do not want to undercut that with an ambiguous political settlement. And so it does put the president in a difficult spot."

At the Pentagon, a senior military official said, "Desert Storm continues to swirl on, regardless. We have our plan and we continue to follow it. Round-the-clock air attacks continue."

Apparently, what Bush was actually contemplating at this time was not whether to accept Gorbachev's peace plan, but how to get around it.

Reportedly concerned that the Soviets were about to succeed in arranging a face-saving way for Hussein to withdraw, Bush on the morning of February 22 issued an ultimatum that, according to *Newsweek,* "was meant to be unacceptable."

It gave Hussein "until noon Saturday to do what he must do: begin his immediate withdrawal from Kuwait." Bush said the withdrawal had to be completed within one week and that all prisoners of war had to be released within forty-eight hours. In return, Bush pledged not to attack Hussein's withdrawing forces.

Iraq denounced Bush's ultimatum as "shameful," but didn't specifically reject it. Instead, it accepted the latest Soviet plan, which gave Iraq three weeks to withdraw. But Bush said the Soviet plan fell short of an unconditional Iraqi withdrawal and was therefore "unacceptable to the United States."

Soviet-Iraqi negotiators said they would continue to meet, taking Bush's demands into account. Less than an hour before the noon deadline, Gorbachev called Bush one last time to try to get him to compromise. Bush said *nyet:* It was all or nothing.

Either Hussein accepted all twelve of the U.N. resolutions and start his withdrawal within the hour, or dread ground war would commence.

Baghdad ignored the noon deadline, and eight hours later the ground war was underway.

In Baghdad, Saddam Hussein informed his country in an angry radio address that the U.S.-led coalition had "stabbed us in the back," and called on his army to "fight them and show no mercy."

He said that "the despicable Bush, his filthy agent [Saudi King] Fahd, and others who have consorted with them in committing crimes, shame, and aggression, were collaborators in treason."

Hussein then forecast a sad future for his nation of seventeen million people should its army be defeated.

"God forbid, there will only a deep abyss into which the enemies are aspiring to push you . . . and an unending darkness will loom over Iraq."

For once during the long crisis, Hussein's prediction proved to be accurate.

The Mother of All Retreats

As hundreds of thousands of allied forces poured into Kuwait, the administration admitted that Bush and a small circle of his advisers had known for almost two weeks the date and hour the assault would begin.

All the last-minute Soviet diplomacy had little effect on the timing of the attack, officials were quoted as saying.

After telling the nation in a televised speech that he had ordered the ground invasion on Saturday night, February 23, Bush went for a solitary walk around the south grounds of the White House with his dog, Ranger, which had replaced first lady Barbara Bush's dog Millie as his favorite.

The next morning, the president, his family, and his closest aides attended a private service at St. John's Episcopal Church— the "Church of the Presidents"—across Lafayette Park from the White House.

Then he went home and waited for news of how the battle was going.

It was going swimmingly, as it turned out—and not in the allies' blood, as Hussein had promised.

In the largest such assault in history, more than three hundred attack helicopters of the 101st Airborne Division had blasted deep into western Iraq in an attempt to cut Hussein's supply lines. Surprisingly, the 101st encountered minimal Iraqi resistance. At the same time, two columns from the U.S. Second Marine Division pushed thirty-five miles north from the frontier.

Meanwhile, the tanks of the First Armored Division rolled across Iraqi territory with a growing sense of elation at the lack of enemy fire. The division was supposed to regroup before facing the elite Republican Guard to the east, but at the scheduled halting point, U.S. troops could see guard units in full retreat. So the First Armored roared right after them.

By the end of the day, U.S. paratroopers were on the outer edges of Kuwait City.

It soon became clear that this was not a ground war. It was, as it quickly became known, "the mother of all retreats." Allied forces were crushing anything that stood in their way, which wasn't much. Iraqi troops were surrendering by the thousands without even trying to put up a fight.

"It's the most incredible thing I've ever seen," one officer told reporters. "Every soldier I saw surrendered."

Some surrendered to reporters. One group even tried to surrender to an unmanned reconnaissance drone.

But during the second day of action, just as the desert duel was turning into a desert debacle for Hussein, the Iraqis scored a direct hit with a Scud missile attack on a U.S. barracks in Dhahran, Saudi Arabia. The missile demolished a barracks housing about one hundred American soldiers, killing twenty-eight of them.

In one moment, a single Scud had inflicted more casualties on the U.S. military than had hundreds of thousands of Iraqi troops and thousands of tanks in two days of ground combat.

And where were the much-praised Patriot missiles at the time of the attack? On June 5, 1991, the Army blamed their failure to react on a computer problem that had been detected five days before the Scud. The Army added that the software to correct the problem had arrived the day before the attack but hadn't been installed.

Iraq also fired its first Scud at Qatar, an Arab member of the multinational coalition. But the missile crashed in a deserted area and no damage was reported.

American losses were reported as "extremely light," excluding those caused by the Scud attack. Four Americans were reported killed and twenty wounded, the U.S. command said. It also reported the loss of four U.S. aircraft, but said three of the four pilots had been rescued.

Also on Day 2 of the ground assault, Kuwaiti resistance leaders declared that they were in control of their homeland's smoke-filled capital after almost seven months of Iraqi occupation. But they warned that fleeing Iraqi troops had taken thousands of Kuwaiti captives with them and had left behind an armory of tanks and loaded weapons.

To try to prevent further embarrassment, Hussein ordered his troops to withdraw from Kuwait at the end of the second full day of the ground assault.

But that wasn't good enough for Bush. Clearly considering Hussein's personal humiliation every bit as important as the U.N.-mandated objective of liberating Kuwait, the White House demanded that the Iraqi leader "personally and publicly" agree to an unconditional withdrawal before it would order an end to the allied offensive.

"We will not attack unarmed soldiers in retreat," press secretary Marlin Fitzwater said while coalition troops apparently were firing on Iraqis matching that description. "But we will consider retreating combat units as a movement of war."

Many Iraqi soldiers interviewed after the war said they were shocked when Hussein issued the withdrawal order. Some said they also were angry because they received no explanation for the decision.

"We were puzzled and shocked when we were told we had to withdraw," a young Republican Guard soldier told the Associated Press. He said the withdrawal started chaotically.

Another Iraqi soldier was quoted as saying that troops had abandoned their weapons in an "unorganized, speedy retreat" that amounted to "a race against time and death."

"During our retreat we were being shot at and bombed by the American fighter planes," he told AP. He said the only way to survive was to "hide when the American planes fired, and run before the next planes returned."

Three weeks later, the *Los Angeles Times* gave one reason why the allied operation had gone so smoothly: New evidence indicated that, while allied bombs had killed far fewer Iraqi soldiers than previously estimated, they had caused enemy troops to desert in such large numbers that some defensive lines were left virtually unmanned.

The *Times* quoted senior officers as saying that at least 200,000 Iraqi soldiers were believed to have fled their positions during the five weeks of the intense air campaign that preceded the ground attack. That would mean that two Iraqis in five had deserted by the time the ground war began.

"What was telling about the air campaign was the psychological effect that it had on [Hussein's] soldiers," Brig. Gen. Steven Arnold, chief of operations for Army forces in the gulf, was quoted as saying.

Lt. Col. Raymond Cole said his First Marine Division had found Iraqi logs showing that "some units . . . were defeated even before they were attacked."

According to postwar estimates, the rate of desertion among Iraqi soldiers had reached 40 percent during the air campaign, indicating that the quick victory by allied ground forces was won over an enemy numbering 312,000 troops instead of the expected 520,000.

Another reason for the rout, *Newsday* reported, was that the Iraqi military never prepared detailed battle plans against an allied invasion because it knew it couldn't win and believed Hussein would reach a last-minute political settlement.

Newsday quoted a U.S. official who had just returned from the Persian Gulf and was familiar with the debriefings of senior Iraqi officers who were prisoners of war: "The [Iraqi] general officers knew they couldn't win the war and weren't planning to fight a war. They didn't expect to fight a war because they knew damn well they'd be creamed."

The Iraqi officers "assumed Saddam was playing a game of chicken and would turn off the road at the last minute or reach a political compromise," the unnamed official said.

The official added that military planners in Baghdad also failed to draft contingency plans to counter an offensive by the allies if the "game of chicken" failed.

By inference, *Newsday* said, Hussein himself appeared not to have believed the allies would attack or he would have ordered the drafting of war plans tailored to meet an allied offensive—if not to win, to at least make it a costly victory for the coalition.

One of the few exceptions to the lack of planning and initiative by the Iraqi military was the torching of Kuwaiti oil wells, which the Iraqis hoped—incorrectly, as it turned out—would create a smoke screen against allied bombing attacks.

Despite the early reports of success, though, the military command cautioned that more than a week of tough fighting, possibly including house-to-house combat in Kuwait City, might lie ahead.

A Russian Riposte

As the ground war raged, the Soviet Union coldly complained that Bush had launched the offensive just when a peace settlement appeared imminent. Defense Minister Dmitri Yazov also charged that the United States was exceeding the U.N. mandate by bombing Iraqi cities. And foreign ministry spokesman Vitaly Churkin said "the instinct to rely on a military solution prevailed" even though Iraq had agreed to withdraw its forces from Kuwait.

An official statement issued by the Kremlin noted that just before the ground war, Iraqi and U.S. positions had been closer than at any time since the crisis had begun in August, "and lent themselves to resolution." The statement gave several examples:

• Iraq would withdraw within a three-week period. The United States would give it no more than a week.

• Iraq would release the POWs in three days. The United States wanted immediate release—a requirement it didn't enforce even after the cease-fire was implemented.

• Iraq wanted the United Nations to drop all anti-Iraq resolutions, including economic sanctions, demands for war reparations, and a ban on arms sales. The United States refused.

And so it went. The war obviously was now being fought over quibbling points. Clearly, the object was not to liberate Kuwait. It was to humiliate Saddam Hussein.

Yet allied nations strongly backed the U.S.-led ground assault.

British Prime Minister John Major, whose country had created so many of the war's precipitating irritants for its own greedy gain in the 1920s, said with a dignity reminiscent of his colonialist forebears that he was "absolutely convinced that there is no choice" but to continue the ground war until Iraq was forced from Kuwait.

In Germany, Chancellor Helmut Kohl declared "firm and inviolable support" for the assault—as long his his nation's hands didn't have to get any blood on them.

The Kuwaiti ambassador to London, Ghazi Al-Rayes, thanked the allies "for liberating my country." As a member of the royal family, Al-Rayes could properly call Kuwait "my country." But he and his family were about to be shocked to learn that the long-disenfranchised common Arabs who had stayed in Kuwait and organized an effective resistance force had decided that it was *their* country, too.

Many newspapers, which generally appeared to have swiftly surrendered their skepticism and professional standards to government-induced war hysteria, joined their governments in blaming Hussein for what the Sydney, Australia, *Daily Telegraph Mirror* called "bloody arrogance."

The *Straits Times* in Singapore agreed. "The ground war signals the allied powers' determination not to let Iraq, and its shifty friends, snatch a political victory from the jaws of almost certain military defeat," the paper said.

But there was uneasiness among others that Bush's military solution might go beyond restoring Kuwait's sovereignty—as provided for in resolutions passed by the U.N. Security Council— to getting rid of Hussein.

"The United States should refrain from conducting military actions that might lead to an expanded interpretation of the U.N. resolutions," said the *Japan Economic Journal*. "We should not make this ground war 'the war for Americans,' instead of the benefit of the U.N.'s function to maintain peace."

When Hussein ordered his forces to withdraw from Kuwait, he still managed to maintain his rhetorical flourish:

> Oh great people, oh nobles in the forces of *jihad* and faith, oh glorious men of the mother of battles, oh truthful zealous believers in our glorious nation and all Muslims and good people in the world, oh glorious Iraqi women:
>
> In such circumstances and moments, it is difficult to say all that should be said. . . . Nevertheless, it is necessary to mention the essential.
>
> This day, our armed forces will complete their withdrawal from Kuwait. Today, our fight against aggression and atheism

in a thirty-country coalition that has officially waged a U.S.-led war on us, will have lasted from the night of January 16 and 17 until this moment—two months of the legendary showdown.

This showdown is a clear evidence of what God meant it to be: a lesson that would lead the believers to faith, immunity, and capability, and the unfaithful, criminals, traitors, evil, and depraved, to abyss, weakness, and humiliation.

As most of Hussein's troops withdrew in what soon became pure panic, Pentagon officials continued to insist the Iraqis were not withdrawing but retreating, and could fight later.

"We must continue to prosecute the campaign until we are absolutely sure that any withdrawal is true both in letter and spirit," one official said. "If a single American life is lost in a ruse, that would be a tragic thing."

Bush declared that the war would go on. "Saddam is not interested in peace, but only to regroup and fight another day," he said.

Next to the Iraqis, the biggest losers were the pool reporters who followed the rules and continued to accompany U.S. ground forces. Few were able to file dispatches that arrived in the United States in time for that day's evening news or the next day's morning newspaper. The much-maligned pool system, in which reporters with individual units filed stories, photos, and television and radio tape for use by all news organizations, had simply collapsed.

The big winners, on other hand, were the reporters who couldn't or wouldn't wait. Because they hadn't been granted pool status, Forrest Sawyer of ABC, Bob McKeown of CBS, and John King of the Associated Press had little to lose when they ran a highway obstacle course north to Kuwait City on February 26.

As it turned out, Americans would have known little or nothing about how the Iraqis had almost totally abandoned the capital city if it hadn't been for the nonpool reports.

As McKeown, with the aid of a portable satellite uplink, was interviewing joyous Kuwaiti citizens in the heart of the capital, the military briefer in Riyadh was telling reporters that "portions of the Iraqi army are still in Kuwait, including Kuwait City. They remain a threat to our coalition forces and to the Kuwait City populace."

Nor was there any sign that the uncensored reports filed by nonpool reporters were breaching military security.

"They're not creating problems," Pentagon spokesman Pete Williams admitted.

When the ground offensive began on February 24 and the Pentagon announced a news blackout and stopped providing information, hundreds of reporters decided to head out on their own.

By February 26, CBS and ABC each had two crews out on their own, equipped with portable satellite dishes. NBC had one and CNN at least three. Several major American newspapers, as well as the Associated Press, also had nonpool reporters in the field. The most timely and riveting material for the most part came from these correspondents.

From Rout to Massacre

The end of offensive ground action came after a tank battle in southern Iraq destroyed any serious threat from the vaunted Republican Guard.

Iraq's elite forces were routed in what was called the largest tank battle since World War II. But one Pentagon source said the Republican Guard tanks "never fought the way you thought a division would fight. We just kind of chased them across the plains, shooting at them."

Allied forces poured it on with a vengeance that some in the West would later question and those in the Mideast would denounce.

During the final hours of the hundred-hour offensive, the U.S. Navy's Silverfox bombing squadron dropped beneath low cloud cover in northern Kuwait and southern Iraq, found itself above more than 1,500 Iraqi tanks, armored vehicles, jeeps, Kuwaiti water and fuel tankers, ambulances, firetrucks, tractor-trailers, and passenger cars all heading to Iraq.

Even though some of the vehicles were flying white flags, the squad didn't hesitate to take advantage of what one member would later describe as "a turkey shoot."

Before it was over, Navy, Air Force, and Marine pilots had trapped the miles-long convoy by disabling vehicles at its front and rear, then pounded it for hours with anti-personnel bombs, and finally finished it off with devastating B-52 bombing runs. Hundreds or perhaps thousands of Iraqi troops were crushed or incinerated in their vehicles.

They were, a squadron leader would later admit to reporters, "just sitting ducks." Another pilot said it was "like shooting fish in a barrel."

Afterward, several hundred charred vehicles and dozens of bodies filled the fifty-mile stretch of highway. Reporters would later discover that another fleeing convoy had been destroyed in a similar fashion along a second road that connects Kuwait to Iraq.

The ferocity of the bombing on the "highway of death," its timing, and public presentation by U.S. military officers constituted one of the war's most disturbing episodes.

While the highway bombing was an act of war ordered by allied field commanders seeking to protect their troops, the *Washington Post* reported that it was also part of a public-relations campaign designed to demonstrate the nearly total destruction of Iraq's army in Kuwait.

"We want to keep it [the war] going. . . . This guy [Hussein] cannot be trusted," Knight-Ridder Newspapers quoted an official in Washington as saying. The U.S. objective at that point, the official added, was "to keep after his military until it is thoroughly defeated."

Pilots from the *USS Ranger* aircraft carrier later admitted to the *Post* that they had hit the convoy again and again—like sharks in a feeding frenzy—dropping cluster bombs and whatever else they could quickly load onto their planes as the *William Tell Overture* blasted from every speaker on every deck. Marine fighters dropped 500-pound bombs on the vehicles, and Air Force fighter-bombers raced north from bases in Saudi Arabia to join in the fun.

There were so many planes striking the convoy, pilots said, that the "killing box" had to be divided in half by air traffic controllers to avoid mid-air collisions.

Later, some of the pilots below said they were amazed by the scale of the destruction. A few even said they felt pity for the Iraqis. But most said they thought the Iraqis had got what they deserved.

"I think we're past the point of just letting [Hussein] get in his tanks and drive them back into Iraq and say 'I'm sorry,'" a U.S. Air Force pilot told a pool reporter as he rested between missions. "I feel fairly punitive about it."

A Navy pilot, speaking to a reporter on the *Ranger* as he reloaded between attacks on the highway, said "one side of me says, 'That's right, it's like shooting ducks in a pond.' Does that make me uncomfortable? Not necessarily. Except there is a side of me that says, 'What are they dying for? For a madman's cause? And is that fair?' Well, we're at war. It's the tragedy of war. But we do our jobs."

But Iraq's Arab friends expressed horror and outrage.

"It's a slaughter," Zaki M. Ayoubi, a Jordanian businessman and consultant, told a reporter after reading about the bombing. "You are going to slaughter 100,000 young men, who belong to 100,000 families. We're not talking abstract artillery and machinery."

Libya's official news agency quoted Foreign Minister Ibrahim Mohamed al-Bishari as saying the allied coalition was exceeding its U.N. authority by killing Iraqis in retreat.

"After Iraq's decision to completely and unconditionally withdraw from Kuwait, it is unacceptable to continue to chase Iraq and pursue the war against it," Bishari told the ambassadors of France, Italy, and Spain in Tripoli. "The Arab people of Libya will not bear it or accept it."

Pro-Iraq demonstrations were reported in Egypt, Algeria, and Morocco.

The *Post* later reported that while the bombing was underway, U.S. officials were deliberately downplaying evidence that Iraqi troops were actually leaving Kuwait after Hussein's withdrawal announcement. Instead, they emphasized that Iraqi forces had had to abandon their weapons and armor only after allied attacks, then argued that Iraqi troop movements were not a voluntary withdrawal but a retreat under fire.

When a military briefer was asked about reports of the highway massacre, he acknowledged that the air campaign was being pressed with full force, but repeated that "there's no significant Iraqi movements to the north." But by noon Tuesday, interviews with U.S. attack pilots conducted by media pool reporters had undercut the briefer's version of events.

Actually, most Iraqi troops in and around Kuwait City had begun to flee on Monday night.

As the day wore on, the *Post* reported, officers with the U.S. Central Command became worried about what they saw as a growing public perception that Iraq's forces were leaving Kuwait voluntarily and that allied pilots were bombing them mercilessly. The officers finally agreed that U.S. spokespersons should describe in strong terms Iraq's "withdrawal" as a fighting retreat, or risk turning public opinion against them.

To make sure that point sank in, Bush himself read a brief

televised statement arranged on short notice in which he stressed that the war would continue despite Baghdad's withdrawal announcement.

"Saddam's most recent speech is an outrage," a tough-talking Bush said. "He is not withdrawing. His defeated forces are retreating. He is trying to claim victory in the midst of a rout. And he is not voluntarily giving up Kuwait."

Vice President Dan Quayle—who, according to numerous accounts, had pulled strings to avoid service in the Vietnam War—was at Bush's side during the statement and later made clear that the United States had wanted to render Hussein powerless. "Saddam and his military machine are simply incompatible with a lasting and just peace," Quayle, suddenly a military expert, said in a speech at McGuire Air Force Base in New Jersey.

Bush's statement was followed by a televised military briefing from Saudi Arabia, which had been delayed to accommodate his remarks.

At the briefing, Brig. Gen. Richard Neal emphasized that Iraqi forces were not withdrawing unilaterally, but were being pushed from the battlefield.

"Saddam Hussein has described what is occurring as a withdrawal," Neal said. "By definition, a withdrawal is when you pull your forces back, not under pressure by the attacking forces. Retreat is when you're required to pull your forces back as required by the action of the attacking forces. The Iraqi army is in full retreat."

Yet, according to many accounts, thousands of Iraqi soldiers in and around Kuwait City had begun to pull away more than thirty-six hours before allied ground forces arrived.

A recently retired intelligence officer who reviewed a computer-enhanced radar image of the Iraqi columns told *Newsday* that they appeared to have been on full withdrawal and not on tactical retreat. According to *Newsday*'s Knut Royce and Timothy M. Phelps, who did some of the best reporting on the war from

Washington, the retired officer said the continuous columns indicated that the troops had made no "efforts to conceal or defend, to preserve the force." He added that, had the Iraqis wanted to conceal their movement, "they would have moved in smaller groups, dispersed the movement." He said they also would have created flanks to protect the columns.

The *Newsday* report also noted that many of the targets were not military vehicles, even though Rear Adm. Ronald Zlatoper, commander of the *USS Ranger* battle group, had told his pilots not to hit nonmilitary targets. "Our job is to take out Iraqi armor and armored personnel carriers and not buses," Zlatoper had said at the time.

But, Royce and Phelps reported, "still photographs and television film of one section of highway just north of Kuwait indicate that there, at least, the planes had done exactly that."

They wrote that the overwhelming majority of the vehicles in the photos were cars, buses, and military and civilian trucks apparently carrying Iraqi soldiers and some civilians. Less than 10 percent of the vehicles in the one section were tanks, personnel carriers, or artillery.

Chuck Myers, a retired military pilot and former deputy undersecretary of defense in charge of air warfare, told Royce and Phelps that while fleeing tanks or artillery might be fair game, there did not appear to be any need to attack the soldiers.

"Why you're beating up on rows of hundreds of thousands of people that are fleeing, I don't understand. I don't know the military value of it. It's not clear," he said.

While the number of people who died amid the wreckage will probably never be known—coalition forces buried the Iraqis in mass graves before most reporters reached the scene—one administration source with access to intelligence reports told Royce and Phelps that on the highway "it is safe to assume that the casualties were massive."

A few days after the "turkey shoot," U.S. soldiers cleaning up the highway carnage said they were satisfied that justice had been done.

"It was like a robbery," one said. "It was like we were the police force and these guys got caught trying to burglarize a house."

Many, indeed, had been thieves in the end. Many of the trucks and police cars were filled with stuffed toys, vacuum cleaners, silverware, soap, even underwear. But burglary isn't a capital offense.

At a March 14 press conference in which he bragged that the war against Iraq marked "the first time in history that a field army has been defeated by air power," the Air Force chief of staff, Gen. Merrill McPeak, defended the highway air attacks.

"You have to understand a little bit about military history," McPeak said. "The true fruits of victory are best exploited while the enemy retreats in disorder. If we do not exploit victory, the president should get himself some new generals. . . . It's a tough business, but our obligation is to our own people. . . . It often causes us to do brutal things. That's the nature of war."

The alternative is to attack only when the foe is ready, he said, and that can prolong a war and increase casualties.

The day before, when Bush was asked at a news conference in Martinique if he had any thoughts that the destruction of the vehicles on the roads between Kuwait City and Basra had been allowed to get out of hand, he bluntly replied, "No, none at all."

But *Newsday's* Royce and Phelps said that outside analysts, diplomats, and even some military officials were beginning privately to express discomfort at what was increasingly looking like a massacre.

"It was an outrage," they quoted a senior Air Force analyst as saying. "They were whipped."

Newsday also reported that some foreign and American diplomats said the United States might pay in the future for killing soldiers who hadn't been fighting.

"Many of those soldiers trying to get away probably had ten or eleven children," a Soviet diplomat who specializes in the Middle East was quoted as saying. "And every one of those children is now a potential anti-American militant."

"Kuwait Is Liberated"

In Kuwait City, the U.S. Marines who had routed Iraq's army rode triumphantly past thousands of jubilant residents as Kuwaiti flags fluttered over the capital for the first time in seven months. Kuwaitis cheered, fired their rifles into the air, and shouted "Thank you, U.S.A!"

The next day, Bush announced that "Kuwait is liberated, Iraq's army is defeated," and announced that at midnight Eastern Standard Time, "all United States and coalition forces will suspend offensive combat operations."

In a televised address, Bush warned the fighting would begin anew if Iraq's forces—shattered and in retreat—fired on allied troops or launched Scud missiles at Israel or Saudi Arabia.

"This war is now behind us," Bush said. "Ahead of us is the difficult task of securing a potentially historic peace."

World leaders and ordinary citizens alike hailed the cease-fire, then began to total its costs in blood, money and hatred.

At least 322 American troops were killed in the war. Another 339 were wounded, and ten were missing in action. Iraqi casualties were far higher, with estimates ranging well above a hundred thousand. But allied commanders refused to provide any count of Iraqi war dead.

Continuation of the cease-fire was contingent on the termination of Iraqi attacks—in the war zone or with missiles—and other conditions, including the immediate release of prisoners of war and any captured civilians.

Iraq's army was in a shambles, destroyed by the four-day ground offensive and the relentless five-and-a-half-week air assault that had preceded it.

At the end, "There was nothing between us and Baghdad," said Operation Desert Storm commander Gen. H. Norman Schwarzkopf. He said the allies could have walked into the Iraqi capital unmolested, but had had no intention of conquering Iraq. Leaving it in ruins and allowing Hussein the job of putting it back together were apparently politically preferrable.

Kuwaitis, in the chilly dawn of their first full day of freedom, tempered their rejoicing as they surveyed the ruins of their reclaimed country.

"It's a catastrophe. It's indescribable," one man told reporters as he gazed at Kuwait City's once-elegant waterfront, disfigured by twisted barbed wire and Iraqi fortifications.

Even as many were celebrating, however, others were continuing to come forward with accounts of torture and terrorism during the seven-month Iraqi occupation.

Medhat M. Farghaly, a surgeon at the Adan Hospital, said that at least a hundred bodies of Kuwaiti men, many bearing signs of torture, had passed through the hospital's morgue since the invasion.

"They have their hands tied behind their backs," he said. "Some have been shot in the back of the head, others show signs of water or air having passed through the anus, and we have seen swollen scrotums, meaning they have been beaten in the testicles."

At the Mubarak Hospital morgue, doctors said the fifty mutilated bodies they received were only a small portion of the victims. "I saw five hundred bodies on my duty alone," said Habra Ahmad, a twenty-year-old Somali who had begun volunteer work with the Red Crescent Society after the invasion.

She pointed to the latest victims: a 12-year-old child, a man who had been burned alive, and several people whose ears had been severed. Many had been shot in the mouth.

Kuwaitis said the Iraqis had performed summary killings and applied torture for at least a month after the occupation. The Iraqis eased up for several months, but resumed with a vengeance after the war started, they said.

But many of these stories later seemed to have been greatly exaggerated. In early April, for example, Middle East Watch, a New York-based human rights group, said evidence suggested the deaths numbered between three hundred and six hundred, not twenty-five thousand, as had been claimed.

The organization also said a widely circulated story that was repeated by President Bush that Iraqi troops had killed hundreds of premature babies by stealing their incubators had proved "totally false."

Kuwaitis also grieved over the casualties and destruction caused by allied bombing, and said the Iraqi invasion seemed to have been motivated by plunder as much as politics.

Witnesses told reporters that the looting began with the most obvious targets, such as the city's gold shops and jewelry stores. By the end, the Iraqis were even stripping carpet from floors and stealing light fixtures.

Commanders were reported to have rewarded their troops by letting them raid specific homes. Often, they just knocked on the door and said, "Give us your keys. We want your car."

But the Kuwaitis fought back as best they could. Many told reporters that they hid their cars in basements, on rooftops, or in empty swimming pools, where they were covered with trash.

Overall, though, the damage done to Kuwait by Iraqi soldiers turned out to be less severe than first reported, according to the *New York Times*. The paper quoted Kuwait's finance and planning ministers as saying that many of the country's highways and bridges were in surprisingly good shape.

The same could not be said of Iraq, where a U.N. mission reported in late March that the war had had "near-apocalyptic results." The damage was so great, it added, that "the Iraqi people may soon face a further imminent catastrophe, which could include epidemic and famine, if life-supporting needs are not rapidly met."

Baghdad Radio signed on the first day of the cease-fire with patriotic songs and its usual denunciation of Iraq's "criminal invaders." It didn't mention the halt in hostilities. But later, a military communique was read announcing the suspension of allied attacks and telling Iraqi troops to respond in kind.

"We are happy for the halt in fighting, which will save a lot of our sons and grant the safety of our people," it said. "Therefore, orders were issued to all our units in the battlefront not to open fire."

To help make sure they were aware of the cease-fire, the allies dropped leaflets on Iraqi troops and blasted the news over loudspeakers in Arabic. Iraqi troops in the battlefield were being allowed to make their way home.

"If they come up to U.S. positions and do not attack U.S. positions then our policy now is to allow them to pass with their weapons," a U.S. military official said.

Most credit for the allied victory, almost everyone agreed, had to go to the U.S. commander, Gen. Schwarzkopf, whose name had become a household word.

Schwarzkopf was known by few outside military circles in 1988, when he took over as chief of U.S. Central Command, a Florida-based headquarters charged with protecting U.S. interests the Persian Gulf region.

With supposedly remarkable foresight, Schwarzkopf was said to have put his staff through a war-game exercise a month before Iraq's invasion of Kuwait that began with a big-time threat to U.S. interests by a small-time dictator in the Middle East. Schwarzkopf's scenario, which required a rapid and large military commitment, was played out just four days before Hussein invaded Kuwait. Within a week, the exercise was serving as the basis for the biggest deployment of U.S. forces abroad since Vietnam.

For Hussein's army, which had started the war as the fourth largest in the world, there was now open derision.

Instead of the battle-hardened force many had called it, the Iraqi army turned out to be battle-weary. It was sizable, but much of it was poorly trained.

The air war waged by the allies had had much to do with the Iraqi army's collapse. So, most analysts agreed, did Hussein's tight rein on his generals. Hussein was notorious for purging or killing officers whose loyalty was suspect, and he permitted few of them to go abroad for training.

But some Americans weren't quite sure that America's victory came about because its leaders were so great and Iraq's so mediocre.

One such skeptic was Mike Royko, who has long been considered by many to be the best daily columnist in the country. After the war ended, Royko wrote:

> Maybe I dozed off and missed it, but of all the retired generals and military analysts on the tube, did even one of them say that in four days the world's fourth-most-powerful fighting force would be looking and acting like haggard recruits on their first day in boot camp? And the loss of American lives would be fewer than we suffered in a routine World War II skirmish?
>
> As a matter of fact, someone did predict it. . . . On January 15, long before the ground war began, an article appeared on the op-ed page of the *Chicago Tribune*. It was written by Professor John J. Mearsheimer, chair of the political science department at the University of Chicago, and a military scholar. . . .
>
> Here are portions of the professor's prophetic article: "The campaign should be over in a week or less and probably fewer than 1,000 Americans will die in combat, a very low number for a large army fighting in a major armored war."
>
> Why would it be that quick and decisive? Mearsheimer

pointed out that our forces are better equipped, better trained in armored warfare and that we controlled the skies.

In contrast: "The Iraqi army . . . is a Third World military that is incapable of fighting mobile armored battles. This crucial Iraqi shortcoming in tank warfare was demonstrated often in the recent Iran-Iraq War, a conflict in which the manifest deficiencies of the Iraqi military were laid bare.

"In fact, even by Third World standards, the Iraqi army is a below-average fighting force. It is certainly not in the same league as the North Vietnamese army, and it does not even measure up well to the Egyptian and Syrian armies. If the Israelis can consistently score impressive victories over the Egyptians and Syrians, even after being completely surprised in 1973, why should we not expect the U.S. military to rout the Iraqis?"

He then explained the ground strategy that would probably be used, and it was pretty close to the strategy that was used.

And he concluded: "Saddam Hussein should understand that the American military is going to inflict a devastating defeat on his military forces in Kuwait. He will be left in much the same position that Gamal Abdel Nasser was in after Israel destroyed his army in the Six-Day War. The American public, on the other hand, should recognize that although there is certainly cause to be concerned about casualties, the United States is not about to become involved in a war of attrition with high casualty levels.

"In fact, American forces may suffer as few as 500 fatalities, roughly the same number of troops the Israelis lost against Egypt and Syria in the Six-Day War."

The professor's uncanny accuracy raised some serious questions, Royko said:

If a University of Chicago professor knew that the supposedly ferocious Iraqi army was "even by Third World standards . . . a below-average fighting force," didn't our vast intelligence establishment know it?

And if they knew it, why were we told, over and over again, that Iraq was not merely a menace to Kuwait and Saudi Arabia, but the entire Arab region?

Newsday columnist Sydney Schanberg, who had courageously poked holes into the war's facade from the beginning, raised another question:

Now that the war with former friend Iraq is over, I wonder whether President Bush will take our troops to Cambodia to wipe out yet another embarrassment. I speak of the Khmer Rouge, like Iraq a foul regime the United States has aided even though Pol Pot's genocidal atrocities make Saddam Hussein look like a wimp.

It was only a thought. I know Bush isn't going after the Khmer Rouge. They're the creatures of our good friends, the dictators of China—and Bush wants to keep the dictators of China happy, no matter how many students they slaughter.

To get back to the Khmer Rouge, who saw to the deaths of perhaps two million Cambodians between 1975 and 1979, Bush says he doesn't like them, but he likes the Vietnamese less. The Vietnamese are the ones who drove the Khmer Rouge out of power in Cambodia in 1979. . . .

Washington gives aid to the two noncommunist guerrilla groups that are part of that coalition with the Khmer Rouge. . . . The Khmer Rouge and the noncommunist factions conduct joint military operations against the Cambodian government, with the Khmer Rouge as the dominant force. And yet [their] White House pals brazenly have kept shouting that the non-communist guerrillas always fought independently and never in coordination with the Khmer Rouge. Therefore, said these sanctimonious hypocrites, the United States had not—not ever, not even indirectly or remotely—given the slightest smidgen of aid or comfort to the Khmer Rouge.

So they've said—until this week. Because Tuesday, the White House made a stunning admission to Congress. Yes, the White House conceded, the noncommunist guerrillas we support sometimes fight in joint operations alongside the Khmer Rouge. . . .

Let's see if I understand this. These groups work together— our side and the guys who slaughtered the Cambodian people— but our side doesn't help them. They help us. Should we send them a letter of thanks? Excuse me, Mr. President, is this the new world order?

But most Americans weren't nearly so critical. Exactly six weeks after the "the mother of all battles" had started, most Americans were delighted at how it had turned out.

From sea to shining sea, the *Los Angeles Times* reported, the prevailing sentiment was, "Hooray for us! We kicked butt! America the Great! We take no guff from no one no more no how."

As for George Bush, the *Times* said, the tag "wimp" had been buried beneath the desert sand.

"When [Bush] ran for office, I wasn't for him; I always thought he was weak," Mary Baldimar, owner of a small flower shop in Honolulu told the *Times*. She said she thought Bush's wife was the tougher of the two. And now, she said, that made her chuckle.

Apparently it also made a lot of other Americans chuckle too. A *USA Today* poll of 622 adults found 91 percent approval for Bush's handling of the presidency. That was a higher rating than any other president had received since polls began being taken early this century. The survey also found that if Bush ran for re-election at that point, seventy-two percent would vote for him regardless of who ran against him. Only twelve percent would vote for someone else.

So Bush and America stood triumphant. But they were soon to discover that winning the peace was a lot harder than winning the war.

Winning the Peace

Many wars start with little or no time spent beforehand at a peace conference table. But they all end up at one.

So it was with the Persian Gulf War, albeit in the simplest of surroundings. On March 3, 1991, in a tent by an airstrip near Safwan, Iraq, a town of 3,000 people just across the Kuwaiti border, several coalition and Iraqi generals sat around a simple redwood table and discussed how to end the war between their huge military forces.

"This is a historic day," said the U.S. commander and chief delegate, Gen. H. Norman Schwarzkopf.

But it was also meant to be a one-sided day. "I'm not here to give them anything," Schwarzkopf said before entering the two-hour meeting. "I'm here to tell them exactly what we expect them to do."

When the Iraqi delegation of seven generals and a colonel arrived, they looked grim. After members of the two delegations had shaken hands and entered the tent, Schwarzkopf told some jokes to lighten the somber mood. The Iraqis smiled, then they got down to business.

Afterward, Schwarzkopf told a news conference that the Iraqis had agreed to ensure their forces didn't come into contact with U.S. forces.

"I am very happy to tell you we agreed on all matters, Schwarzkopf said. He added that a "symbolic release" of POWs would be made immediately to show good faith, and that "all detainees, including several thousand Kuwaiti civilians being held by Iraq, would be treated as war prisoners."

He said U.S. troops would withdraw from occupied southern Iraq as soon as a permanent cease-fire could be signed and Iraq had complied with U.N. resolutions requiring Baghdad, among other things, to rescind its annexation of Kuwait and accept liability for war damages.

About twelve hours later, Baghdad Radio announced that Iraq has accepted the U.N. conditions, clearing the way for a permanent cease-fire.

It had all been so easy, defeating Iraq. So easy, in fact, that one couldn't help but wonder how Saddam Hussein had ever come to be viewed as the second coming of Adolf Hitler, and his mediocre military machine as a new *Wehrmacht.*

At any rate, as Secretary of State James A. Baker III quickly admitted at the end of the hostilities, winning the peace would be decidedly more difficult.

The peace process would be complicated by three major questions:

• Would Hussein remain in power in Baghdad?

• Would the United States come to be viewed as a colonial power in the mold of Britain and France, whose self-serving creation of the Mideast's political boundaries caused many of the region's subsequent problems?

• Would the Arab nations and Israel be willing to resolve the differences between them that had caused forty years of conflict in this crucial crucible of civilization?

President Bush and his top aides immediately began trying

to use the allied victory to discredit and undermine Hussein, and it didn't take long for that to begin to happen. Just hours after the war between the Allies and Iraq had ended, a war between the Iraqis themselves had begun.

The first action reported was in Basra, where units of the Republican Guard were said to be fighting ferocious battles with Shiite opponents of Hussein, including defeated soldiers arriving from Kuwait.

Anti-Hussein demonstrations were reported during the first postwar weekend in five other eastern Iraqi cities.

U.S. military sources were quoted as saying that seven thousand soldiers were recalled to Baghdad, apparently to protect Hussein.

But Iraq's official voice portrayed Hussein as being in firm control of the government and nation. Baghdad Radio said he had met with the ruling Revolutionary Command Council and the Baath Party Regional Command to discuss "the latest developments in the political situation."

In early March, in his first nationally televised address after the war, Hussein promised political reform, including a new parliament, constitution, and cabinet, in an apparent attempt to trim the sails of the twin revolts against him.

A week later, Hussein kept his word, at least in part. He shuffled his cabinet, but kept his hard-line ministers of interior and defense to direct a crackdown on dissent.

But a Bush administration official was quoted as saying that Hussein "still controls the levers of power."

In the same speech in which he promised reform, Hussein, without mentioning the predominantly Shiite nation by name, accused Iran of fomenting the Shiite rebellion. He referred to the rebels as "stooges and agents of foreign enemies," and said the Kurds were fighting to serve their own interests and those of Zionist Israel.

But Iraqis had a right to be skeptical of Hussein's promise of reform. He had made similar pledges just before his invasion of Kuwait, but the reforms were not carried out.

Bush was dubious, too. "The proof of that pudding is in the eating," Bush said as he continued his verbal volleys against Hussein. "I find it very difficult to see a situation under which we would have normalized relations with Saddam Hussein still in power. His credibility is zilch, zero, zed."

As if to emphasize the point, American troops returned to positions deep inside Iraq to ensure they could control the area until a formal cease-fire agreement was reached.

Though it was officially keeping a hands-off policy toward the fighting in Iraq, the Bush administration was encouraging the insurrection against Hussein's government by limiting his ability to crush it. The downing of two Iraqi warplanes by U.S. jet fighters demonstrated how the administration was using the cease-fire rules it had set at the end of the war to aid the rebels.

The administration also threatened, initially, to shoot down any Iraqi attack helicopters used against Shiite and Kurdish rebels, but then backed off after admitting that part of the cease-fire agreement involved only an oral understanding between Gen. Schwarzkopf and Iraqi military officers.

Bush first raised the helicopter issue at a March 13 press conference in Ottawa with Canadian Prime Minister Brian Mulroney.

"I must confess to some concern about the use of Iraqi helicopters in violation of what our understanding was," Bush said. He added that the issue "has got to be resolved before we're going to have any permanence to any cease-fire. These helicopters should not be used for combat purposes inside Iraq."

Later, Bush told reporters he was "warning" the Iraqis: "Do not do this." But White House spokesman Marlin Fitzwater changed the tone—if not the tune itself—of that message on March 26 when he admitted that combat use of helicopters was "not covered by the terms of the cease-fire," but only by the informal oral agreement Schwarzkopf had with Iraqi commanders.

"This was an understanding that was reached in discussions between Gen. Schwarzkopf [and the Iraqis] and it was a side, oral discussion—nothing in writing," Fitzwater said. "We made it clear that we do not believe that they should be flying helicopters or fixed-wing aircraft over the country, that we intend to shoot down fixed-wing aircraft because of the direct threat that they pose to our forces."

In a PBS interview with David Frost broadcast the next night, Schwarzkopf said he was "suckered" by Iraqi negotiators on the helicopter agreement. He said they told him they needed their helicopters to transport government officials during the cease-fire because U.S.-led bombing missions had destroyed most of Iraq's roads and bridges.

"I think I was suckered because I think they intended . . . to use those helicopters against the insurrections that were going on," Schwarzkopf told Frost.

Schwarzkopf also said Bush had overruled his "recommendation" that U.S. forces "continue the march" in the war. "I mean, we had them in a rout and we could have continued to, you know, reap great destruction upon them. We could have completely closed the door and made it in fact a battle of annihilation," he said. But he said Bush decided instead that "we should stop at a given time, at a given place that did leave some escape routes open for them to get back out, and I think it was a very humane decision and a very courageous decision on his part also."

In the first clash of victory-fed egos, Bush disputed Schwarzkopf's version of events, saying all involved had been in "total agreement" that the time had come to stop the war. In a written statement issued a short time later, Defense Secretary Dick Cheney said Schwarzkopf had "raised no objection to terminating hostilities." He added that both Schwarzkopf and Gen. Colin Powell "were consulted and made the recommendation to me and to the president that we had achieved our military objectives and agreed that it was time to end the campaign." A day later, Bush called Schwarzkopf to tell him not to worry about the embarrassing incident. Schwarzkopf later apologized for his poor choice of words and said he had supported the decision to end the war.

Second Thoughts

But by then a lot of other people were questioning the decision as Hussein escalated his bloody reprisals against civilians in response to the rebellions.

A White House spokesman said that though Bush regretted the suffering resulting from Hussein's violent efforts to end the insurrections, "the issue of internal unrest in Iraq is an issue that has to be settled between the government and the people of Iraq."

Bush's decision not to help the rebels directly reportedly grew out of his hesitance to broaden U.S. involvement into what might become an unseemly and protracted occupation. Vacillation was the administration's general response toward Hussein's attempt to crush the rebellions against him, and tens of thousands of lives were lost as a result.

On the one hand, the administration wanted to see Hussein overthrown. On the other, officials didn't believe the rebels, especially the Shiites, could succeed. In fact, some actually feared the rebellions might work in Hussein's favor by allowing him to solidify his hold on the military, which might otherwise have turned against him.

U.S. officials were also said to have misgivings about the Kurdish rebels' goal of establishing a separate Kurdish state in northern Iraq.

Ultimately, American analysts concluded that a victory by either group would lead to an unstable, divided government at best, and would make it more likely that American troops would have to remain for a lengthy period, officials were quoted as saying.

"Our policy is not to see a Lebanonization of Iraq," State Department spokeswoman Margaret Tutwiler said. "We are not for the dismemberment of Iraq."

But some analysts said this may be exactly what the war gave to the world, as up to twenty rebel factions sought to wrest control of the country from Hussein.

"What we wanted was a strong Iraq without Saddam Hussein," Michael Hudson, professor of international relations at Georgetown University, told the *Boston Globe*. "What we got was a weak Iraq with Saddam Hussein."

The only difference between Iraq and Lebanon appeared to be that the resulting chaos in Iraq was on so large and potentially more dangerous a scale that it could jeopardize the entire region's delicate balance of power.

Meanwhile, Tehran Radio, the official voice of Iran, kept putting a positive spin on the failing Shiite rebellion in its neighbor's south. But Tehran's interest was a lot more than that of a sideline cheerleader. According to *Newsweek,* both Iran and Syria had immediately armed Iraqi exiles after the cease-fire to foment unrest. Iran was reported to have sent three thousand Kurdish and Shiite rebels to Iraq along with trucks loaded with small arms, and it was perhaps not coincidental that it was the Kurds and Shiites who were leading the revolt.

As the rebellion intensified, *Newsweek* reported, at Khorram-shahr, an Iranian border town destroyed during the Iran-Iraq War, trucks full of food and medicine were being dispatched into rebel-held Iraqi territory. Ambulances reportedly also were busy racing toward Iranian hospitals with wounded Iraqi rebels, and armed revolutionists were standing guard at the city library, which had been converted into a headquarters for the Supreme Assembly of the Islamic Revolution, an umbrella group of anti-Hussein Shiites.

A few days later, the *New York Times* quoted officials in Kuwait City as saying that Iran had "embarked on a methodical campaign to unseat Hussein and replace him with a friendly Shiite Muslim government."

The *Times* said the rebels included Shiite soldiers from the Iraqi army captured during the Iran-Iraq War who had remained in Iran, as well as members of Iraqi families of Persian origin who were rounded up by Iraq near the start of the eight-year conflict and deported to Iran.

An editorial in the government-controlled *Tehran Times* left little doubt where the Iranian government stood when the paper called for Hussein's government to be replaced by a "popular government" while warning that the Iraqi military must be kept from taking on a "large or leading role."

Without firing a shot, in fact, Iran—which before Iraq temporarily unseated it had been the United States' most bitter enemy in the region—had emerged as one of the big winners of the Persian Gulf War. And that, experts warned, could spell trouble for the Bush administration's hopes for lasting U.S. influence and order in the region.

Some analysts said that if Hussein and his secular Baath Party were overthrown, Iraq might still wind up with a government dominated by Shiite Muslims, who make up the majority of the diverse nation's population and who might then ally themselves with Iran's Shiite government. That, in turn, could radicalize Shiites in Kuwait, where they they make up almost a third of the population.

Before the war, many experts on the Middle East had warned Bush and his aides that the dismantling of Iraq would create a vacuum that Iran and other rivals would rush to fill.

One State Department consultant on Iraq, who requested that he not be identified, told the author that he didn't know of a single serious student of Iraq who had favored war over sanctions.

"I was telling the State Department from August on that war would only destabilize Iraq and allow Iran to reassert its influence," the analyst said. "But the feeling I got from the beginning was that war was inevitable."

Iran Rises Again

And now that Iraqi influence had been greatly diminished, if not destroyed, Iran was stepping to the fore, just as the Bush administration had been warned. Thanks to the most mysterious episode in the war, Iran was suddenly the proud possessor of some 120 of Iraq's best aircraft, which apparently were flown there for safekeeping during the war.

In addition, Iran had just bought twenty-five MiG-29 fighter jets from the Soviet Union in a deal that called for fifty more, Patrick Clawson of the Foreign Policy Research Institute in Philadelphia told the Associated Press.

But *Newsweek* said fears of a extremist Islamic government in Baghdad might be off-target—or at least premature.

The Tehran-based leader of the "Supreme Assembly" of Iraqi exiles, Ayatollah Muhammad Bakr al-Hakim, reportedly had said he sought not a fundamentalist regime but only free elections to decide Iraq's political future.

"Hakim heads just one group fighting Saddam Hussein," *Newsweek* quoted Iranian Deputy Foreign Minister Abbas Maleki as saying. "There are others more numerous and stronger."

Iran's president, Ali Akbar Hashemi Rafsanjani, had urged Hussein to "submit to the will of the people" and step down, but he had also urged all political groups in Iraq to work together.

The war had also been an economic boon to Iran, which had been able to increase its oil exports as a result of the world boycott of oil from Iraq and Kuwait. As a result, the U.S. government calculated that Iran raised an extra $4 billion from oil sales in 1990, 65 percent more than it would have received otherwise.

By attempting to mediate a peaceful solution to the conflict, Iran also appeared to have improved its world image.

How the country would use its new economic and political power remained to be seen, but it gave an inkling on March 17, when Foreign Minister Ali Akbar Velayati said his nation would soon resume diplomatic ties with Saudi Arabia, ending one of the Islamic world's most bitter feuds. The announcement followed a three-hour meeting between the Iranian minister and his Saudi counterpart, Prince Saud al-Faisal.

Relations between the two nations broke off after Saudi security forces battled rioters during the annual Muslim pilgrimage to Mecca in August 1987, resulting in the deaths of 275 Iranians. Each country blamed the other for the disaster.

In a communique issued after their meeting, the two ministers said they had discussed the annual Muslim pilgrimage as well as other bilateral relations.

Tehran Radio said the restoration of diplomatic relations was assured by agreement between the two countries regarding the number of Iranian pilgrims who would be allowed into Saudi Arabia for the pilgrimage in June. The English-language *Tehran Times* had reported earlier that the Saudis had offered to host 110,000 Iranians, double the number it had permitted in recent years.

Oman, which mediated the talks, was reported to be sympathetic to Iran's arguments against a future U.S. military presence in the region.

The Saudis seemed to be having some second thoughts of their own about U.S. influence. Not that they didn't appreciate the American effort to drive Iraq out of Kuwait and therefore away from their border, but the Saudis also learned that the fruits of victory sometimes have a bitter aftertaste. In their case, victory brought a huge deficit, the prospect of plunging oil revenues, a bigger defense budget, the hatred of the Arab masses, and a citizenry suddenly aware of the concept of freedom.

In dollars and cents, the war's costs were devastating for a country unused to making sacrifices. With a gross national product of about $100 billion a year, the Saudis had suddenly chocked up around $60 billion in war debts. The government's promised payment to the United States of $13.5 billion alone was going to more than devour any windfall oil profits gained by production hikes during the crisis.

After a $15.3 billion deficit in 1990, the Saudis' revenue shortfall was expected to be $32 billion in 1991. Because of the cost of the war, the Saudis sought $3.5 billion in loans from foreign banks— a fact that was played down internally because the Koran prohibits the payment of interest.

As a result, Riyad has become more diplomatically daring itself. Rather than throwing their money around to keep potential enemies happy, the Saudis seemed to be ready to start throwing their weight around instead.

"Everybody who stood up for Saddam Hussein is going to go under with Saddam Hussein," Prince Bandar bin Sultan, Saudi Arabia's ambassador to the United States, said at the war's end. Among his targets were King Hussein of Jordan, whom he called "a goner," and Yasser Arafat of the Palestine Liberation Organization, whom he called "a clown."

Saudi Arabia stopped the cash flow to Jordan and the PLO as soon as each sided with Hussein.

On a more personal level, people from Jordan, Sudan, and Yemen who had enjoyed the relative good life in Saudi Arabia were being given their walking papers because of their governments' support of Iraq.

Many Saudis interviewed by foreign journalists also expressed unease about the moral price the kingdom had paid for its "victory," conducted by outsiders who, even when kept at a distance, brought "subversive" influences with them.

To officials, one of the most worrisome aspects of this was the surfeit of satellite dishes that were bought illegally during the crisis by Saudis starved for the kind of news they could get from CNN but not on the state-run netwoork.

An even bigger worry than uncensored news was other programming that comes in via satellite: "filthy" soap operas from Egypt, shows in Arabic from Israel, radical rhetoric from Syria, and, on occasion, pornography from not-distant-enough Italy.

Possessing or viewing pornography is still a serious offense in puritanical Saudi Arabia. According to the NBC-TV news magazine *Exposé,* one American living and working there was jailed under harsh conditions and tortured for possessing "pornographic" videotapes of the American sitcom *Love Boat.*

But the American was lucky. He got out alive. According to Amnesty International's 1990 annual report, "Torture [in Saudi Arabia in 1989] was reportedly common and one death in custody may have been caused by torture or ill-treatment. Sentences of amputation and flogging continued to be imposed and carried out. At least 111 people were executed, sixteen of them for political offenses."

Not surprisingly, then, King Fahd indicated he was in no more of a hurry to appoint a "consultative council" than the emir was in restoring the Kuwaiti parliament.

With such economic constraints, Saudi Arabia faced the unpleasant choice between continuing its generous and extensive welfare system and buying costly weapons to defend the kingdom against the next Iraq. In the foreseeable future, the Saudis are expected to spend billions of dollars to keep Egyptian and Syrian troops on Saudi soil.

As the euphoria over the defeat of Iraq died down, many Saudis began to express fears about the possibility that their illegal satellite dishes would be confiscated, though some urban liberals still hoped the spread of new sources of information through the closed kingdom would bring a touch of tolerance and pluralism to postwar Saudi society.

"Saudi Arabia is no longer a virgin country," a Riyad businessman was quoted as saying. "We're no longer afraid of exposure. We are conceiving and accepting the point of accelerating change, in a Saudi Arabian way. You'll see a more relaxed Saudi Arabia, a more normalized Saudi Arabia."

But many feared a rapid retreat to prewar rigidity. They noted that since the war ended, state-controlled television has ceased broadcasting CNN, which had been censored to remove all reports from Israel and any news read by anchorwomen dressed too daringly for royal tastes.

In CNN's place is the typical Saudi sampling of prayer, insipid Arabic music videos, more prayer, good news from the government, and more prayer.

Some Islamic fundamentalists claim that the war strengthened their cause by prompting audacious acts like the demonstration staged in November 1990 by forty-three wealthy women who sought to overturn the kingdom's laws prohibiting women from driving.

Although they earned lots of Western media coverage, the women later were subjected to a sharp backlash from the religious right. All lost their jobs and were kept from traveling abroad. But the government's reaction was mild compared with that of the religious establishment, which denounced them from mosque pulpits as "communists," "dirty American secularists," and "advocates of vice."

One flier accused them of having renounced Islam, which can cause you to lose your head while all about you are keeping theirs. A second called upon "every Muslim to cut out the roots of this evil plant before it spreads to every part of our holy land."

Even a visiting member of the U.S. Congress, Representative Beverly B. Byron, a Maryland Democract, had a run-in with the morality police during a postwar visit to Saudi Arabia because she was wearing pants.

The congresswoman told the *Baltimore Sun* that she had been waiting for a colleague at a bazaar in Riyadh when a patrol of Islamic-code enforcers approached her and began tapping the street with their sticks.

Byron said she was surprised when a translator told her the problem, because she thought she had been respecting the strict Muslim culture by wearing a long-sleeved shirt and pants.

"We just walked on," she said, "and that's the end of it." For her, perhaps it was. But it was probably just the beginning for Saudi women in the war's aftermath.

This Is Liberation?

To the north, meanwhile, martial law had been declared, critics said, to quell the threat of rebellion and to keep opposition members from re-entering the country.

A pro-democracy opposition leader was shot and paralyzed, possibly as the first victim of hit squads allegedly hired by the government to kill its foes.

Three men were killed for distributing a banned underground newspaper. The goverment imposed increasing restrictions on journalists, and then stopped foreign reporters from entering the country.

More than forty-five bodies were dumped at local hospitals. Scores of others were beaten, burned, and whipped. Hundreds more were missing.

The country's aloof leader promised democratic reforms, but only after the restoration of order. He had made similar promises in the past, only to renege.

Iraq? No, "liberated" Kuwait.

In the days after the U.S.-led coalition drove Iraqi troops from the tiny emirate on February 26, chaos, revenge, and repression, rather than freedom—to say nothing of democracy—reigned. The plethora of slayings, beatings, and arrests of Palestinians, Iraqis, and others rocked and shocked the land and raised questions not only about who was in control but who *should* be in control.

Things got so bad that Amnesty International, whose report on Iraqi atrocities committed in Kuwait was used by President Bush to rally support for driving the Iraqis out, appealed for protection for those at risk of retaliation from Kuwaitis. "We have received reports that scores of Palestinians, as well as Sudanese and Egyptian nationals, have been arrested in the past few days during house-to-house searches," the respected organization said on March 8.

In addition, the International Red Cross said it was investigating reports that busloads of men, primarily Palestinians, were being dropped off at the Iraqi border after being interrogated and beaten by Kuwaiti police.

"The ones who've been beaten were beaten real bad," one U.S. Army military policeman told a reporter.

Three weeks after Kuwait's liberation, the human-rights group Middle East Watch estimated that Kuwaiti security forces were holding two thousand people, primarily Palestinians, and that hundreds of them had been tortured with knives and lit cigarettes.

The group said secret hospital wards accessible only to Kuwaiti doctors were being used as interrogation and punishment centers by security forces detaining people suspected of collaborating with Iraq during its occupation of Kuwait.

"We have interviewed people who described torture techniques which are very similar to those perpetrated by the Iraqis on the Kuwaitis," said Andrew Whitley, executive director of the New York–based organization.

Whitley told reporters that many, "possibly the majority," of the two thousand people being held had been abused.

Meanwhile, a prominent Kuwaiti banker accused the ruling Sabah family of hiring hit squads to kill leaders of Kuwait's pro-democracy movement. Abdul Aziz Sultan, chairman of the Gulf Bank of Kuwait, said in an interview in early March on ABC-TV's *Nightline* that he had "strong reason to believe" members of the Sabah family had hired assassination squads.

"We do have some hard evidence," Sultan said. "But I'm really not at liberty to divulge that."

The program also included an interview with a hospitalized pro-democracy leader, Hammad al-Johan, who had been shot in his home. *Nightline* also said Scotland Yard had warned a pro-democracy Kuwaiti living in Britain that there was a plot against him by an Irish Republican Army hit man linked to the Sabah family.

A week later, a Western diplomat was anonymously quoted as saying that some members of Kuwait's ruling family had been involved in the killings of Palestinians and other people suspected of collaborating with the Iraqis during the occupation. The high-ranking diplomat had been told by Kuwaiti officials that embarrassed Crown Prince Saad al-Abdallah al-Sabah had threatened to hang six members of his extended family and their "goon squads" unless the random killings and beatings stopped.

Out on the mean streets, meanwhile, the resistance fighters who had helped to feed and organize the mostly less-fortunate 240,000 Kuwaitis left behind after the August 2 invasion said they were being shoved aside by the mostly better-off 400,000 who had fled or had been caught outside the country when the Iraqis invaded.

"We thought society would change," an American-educated dentist was quoted as saying. "But I don't think that anymore."

The resistance fighters also complained about the government's slowness in restoring order and basic services, many of which had been provided by the resistance fighters themselves during the occupation through moxie, hard work, and at great personal risk.

Now officials were telling them to get lost.

Until his low-keyed return, during which he said nothing to the thousands of his subjects who had suffered through seven months of Iraqi occupation, Sheik Jaber al-Ahmed al-Sabah had endured exile with his four wives at the luxurious mountainside resort in Taif, Saudi Arabia, where he set up a government in exile to manage the emirate's $100 billion foreign investments and wage a public-relations campaign to persuade the world to return him to power.

One of the campaign's best arguments was the atrocities committed by the occupying Iraqis. But one American officer who was documenting war crimes described them as "widespread but shallow." The exiled Kuwaiti government frequently claimed that 25,000 citizens were killed or missing. But it turned out that the number was under a thousand.

"There were pockets of intense cruelty," an American officer was quoted as saying. "But we have seen nothing so far that would approach anything close to genocide of the type we saw in World War II."

As it turned out, the reason for the sheik's belated return to his suffering emirate had little to do with security, as had been stated, and a lot to do with making sure he had a fitting place to live.

The effort was given such high priority, in fact, that the first things shipped into Kuwait after its liberation were not food for the hungry, water for the thirsty, medical supplies for the ill and injured, or generators to light the long-darkened city. No, according to the *Nation* and other sources, the first things shipped in by the U.S. Army Corps of Engineers were truckloads of new furniture and gold fixtures of all kinds for Sheik Jaber's restored palace.

Actually, it was for one of the sheik's secondary palaces, since his primary palace had been too badly damaged and was far too large to be restored quickly. And his temporary palace wasn't exactly a palace, either. It was *complex* of palacelike buildings in Kuwait

City, containing a total of more than a hundred plush five-bedroom apartments. Marble dominates each building, right down to the trash cans. Gold is the material of preference for much else. The complex's exterior is dominated by a two-million-gallon water fountain, which, according to columnist Mike Royko, was filled while the emir's parched subjects awaited their first shipment of water.

While it's true Sheik Jabar is no Saddam Hussein and his two-thousand-member ruling family is no brutal Baath Party, he's no Thomas Jefferson, either.

That became obvious a few days after his return, when the first daily newspaper to publish after Kuwait's liberation, called *February 26* for the day the allies expelled the Iraqis, was shut down for running a column criticizing the authorities' failure to restore public services.

Though the emir eventually showed some concern regarding the living conditions of the affluent Kuwaitis who have the right to vote, his response to the rest of the population was brutal repression.

The emirate's two million other residents always had been considered mere foreign laborers, and had few rights. Before the invasion, non-Kuwaitis accounted for 73 percent of the population and 86 percent of the work force—and many of the jobs held by Kuwaitis were little more than an excuse for a government paycheck.

As a result, Kuwaitis made up just 8 percent of the employees in the all-important private sector. It was the non-Kuwaitis who did most of the real work, who dominated the important professions. The British and Americans ran the oil fields. The Palestinians formed the ranks of doctors, lawyers, dentists, engineers, and the middle managers who know how to get things done. The Asians were more likely to be the cooks, gardeners, and nannies. The Bedouin desert nomads, who have no nationality, supplied almost half of Kuwait's

20,000-man military force and most of its police officers.

Many of the hundreds of soldiers who returned to Kuwait from seven months in captivity in Iraq were promptly incarcerated again by the military. Officials told reporters the men would likely be deported in accordance with government policy to cut the number of foreigners in the country.

But the government's plan to reduce the number of non-Kuwaitis by about a million presented major problems, an unavoidable shortage of workers not being the most troublesome.

Kuwait's middle class didn't like the deportation policy, but it would be dangerous for them or the non-Kuwaitis to speak out. Those who have done so in the past have often paid dearly. According to Amnesty International, nearly thirty suspected government opponents were arrested in 1989 alone.

"Of these," Amnesty's 1990 report said, "five were still detained without charge or trial at the end of the year. Twenty-two other suspected government opponents were sentenced to prison terms by the State Security Court after an unfair trial. Seven other political prisoners sentenced after unfair trials in previous years were still held. The death sentence was imposed on at least one person and there was one known execution."

But that was in the good old days. Things aren't likely to be nearly as nice in postwar Kuwait.

Things actually started turning nasty in 1986, when the sheik suspended parliament after politicians complained too much about his policies.

When the complaining started again right after his return, he instructed Crown Prince Saad Al-Salem Al-Sabah to form a new cabinet. But pro-democracy leaders dismissed the change as just another shuffle of ministers.

"Nothing will change," said the opposition's Abdul Aziz Al-Sultan. "We still have the same prime minister. This isn't really a change of people."

But Sheik Jaber didn't have time to listen to such nonsense. Not with the challenge of managing his forty on-again-off-again marriages—he keeps four wives at a time, per Muslim tradition.

(According to the *New York Times,* Sheik Jaber, as often as once a week, is said to marry a young virgin on Thursday night, the eve of the Islamic sabbath, then divorce her on Friday. "All the emir does is get married," the *Times* quoted a prominent Kuwaiti as saying. "Sometimes I think what Saddam Hussein said about these rulers [being immoral] is right.")

Then there are the sheik's seventy children. What's a father to do but give each of the boys an allowance and/or a government department to play with when they come of age? But even that wasn't good enough for one of his sons, who in the 1980s was convicted of writing a bad check and was facing a prison sentence when he fled to Germany. (The sheik's daughters are less of a problem, because Kuwaiti women theoretically know that their place is in the home. But the war helped challenge that tradition, too, and some women took advantage of the postwar chaos to push for greater rights.)

As one of the world's richest men, Sheik Jaber could afford his expensive lifestyle and repressive policies in the past. But it is much more difficult with his country facing $100 billion or more in rebuilding costs and his subjects demanding a bigger piece of the pie.

After all, liberation has its price. And Sheik Jaber probably is beginning to worry about the final bill.

Talking Turkey

Joy wasn't exactly overrunning Turkey, either. President Turgut Ozal had promised great economic and military benefits for Turkey's support of sanctions against Iraq and its decision to permit American aircraft to launch attacks on northern Iraq from air bases there. "For the first time in two hundred years, Turkey has allied itself with the winners of a war," Ozal bragged. "Siding with the winners is always advantageous."

His surfeit of critics, however, wondered if the rewards would be worth the economic and political risks Ozal took. After Iraq invaded Kuwait, Ozal quickly joined the American-led coalition, closed two Iraqi oil pipelines, and cut all other trade with his nation's neighbor. These moves hurt to the tune of an estimated $2 billion when all costs come in.

To show their displeasure, leftist gunmen shot and killed a U.S. businessman at his Istanbul office on March 22, the day Ozal flew to the United States for a weekend meeting with Bush. The gunmen left behind a statement signed by *Dev Sol,* or Revolutionary Left, which said in part, "We are sending Bush, along with Ozal, another Johnny." An American who worked for the same company was killed by gunmen who also claimed membership in *Dev Sol.*

Many in Turkey also expressed fears about Iran's growing influence in the Mideast. But Iran had to play its cards right to keep the situation from backfiring. Demands by Iraqi Kurds for an independent state, for example, could touch off similar demands among the Kurds in Iran, as well as in Syria and Turkey.

"If Lebanonization starts and the Kurds get the upper hand," Hossein Nosrat, a senior editor at the Islamic Republic News Agency, told *Newsweek,* "it means trouble for Iran, too."

But the United States had far less to lose by fomenting rebellion. And so, according to a March issue of *Newsday,* the Bush administration quickly entered into secret talks with Iraqi opposition leaders in exile.

Despite Secretary of State Baker's statement that it was U.S. policy to stay out of Iraq's internal affairs, diplomatic sources were quoted by *Newsday* as saying that the United States was "fully engaged" with the leaders of several of the twenty-three opposition parties and groups that met for three days in Beirut, Lebanon, in mid-March to plan efforts to force Saddam Hussein's ouster and replace him with a democratic government.

In April, the Associated Press quoted intelligence sources as saying that, earlier in 1991, Bush had even signed official orders authorizing the CIA to aid the rebel factions.

The authorizations, if carried out, would have added concrete actions to the verbal encouragement Bush was giving the rebels to overthrow Hussein.

The Associated Press quoted three intelligence sources as saying that Bush signed one or more presidential "findings," as official documents authorizing covert actions are euphemistically called, that broadly described plans to help the rebels.

Six days after the AP report, Kurdish leaders said at a Washington press conference that the CIA had recruited Kurds in Turkey and that a CIA-sponsored radio station had urged the Kurdish people to rise up against Hussein, prompting them to take over many northern towns and cities. They said radio broadcasts began airing from a secret location in January, preaching sedition against Hussein and promising the potential rebels that "we stand by you in whatever you carry out and in every step you take." When it came time to keep that promise, though, the Kurds were left to face the wrath of Hussein as U.S. troops stayed on the sidelines.

But while the United States chose to be discreet about its support of the rebels, the newly repatriated Kuwaitis had no such qualms. Kuwait's ambassador to Lebanon and Syria, Abdel Aziz al-Jassem, promised aid for the movement in a speech at a meeting of exiled Iraqis in Lebanon.

A little American discretion toward the Iraqi rebels didn't mean the United States was going to pull out of the Mideast, however. Defense Secretary Cheney made that clear shortly after the war ended when he said the United States would probably keep an aircraft carrier battle group in the region and maintain a "more robust air presence" there.

Cheney said the Bush administration was not interested in a "large, permanent, long-term U.S. ground presence" in the region. But, in a CNN interview, Cheney said new security measures might be required in the Mideast. "We've crossed a significant threshold there," he noted.

Cheney also warned that while U.S. relations with Persian Gulf states will be closer than in the past, it will be up to leaders of the Arab nations "to take the lead."

"We do not want to impose ourselves in a way that is politically objectionable," Cheney said.

He also said the U.S. victory over Iraq doesn't mean that it must always resort to force in order to settle international difficulties.

"It would be a mistake for us to operate as if we have a dog in every fight—we don't," he said.

But the Chinese and Soviet military establishments aren't so sure. The top brass in both countries are said to be working overtime analyzing America's stunning display of high-tech weaponry and developing crash programs to counter it. That seemed to be confirmed in China on March 26, when leadership announced a sharp increase in military spending despite a rising budget deficit.

The Warrior President

Analysts in both countries, as well as some in the United States, were beginning to see in Bush what they considered a disturbing willingness to use military force as an instrument of policy.

Long before he became president Bush advocated using force with frightening consistency.

He was reported to be openly critical of the reluctance of Reagan and other presidents to show America's military might.

In fact, perhaps the only president to have rivaled Bush in advocating the use of military power was Theodore Roosevelt.

But Americans shouldn't be surprised by Bush's truculence. During the 1988 presidential campaign, he advocated a multi-pronged approach to foreign policy comprising the use of "negotiations, intelligence, economic strength and aid, public diplomacy, and, yes, military power."

Six weeks before the gulf crisis came to a head, in fact, defense correspondent Michael T. Klare reported in the June 18 issue of *Nation* that "the threat posed by Iraq and other well-equipped Third World powers first emerged as a major U.S. concern shortly after the 1988 election. . . . The administration began to identify the emergence of regional powers as a military threat, which eventually would be faced on the battlefield rather than [at] the bargaining table."

According to Klare, this policy was fully articulated by Bush on February 1, 1990, when he said: "We will continue to work hard to prevent this dangerous proliferation [of high-tech weapons]. . . . But one thing is certain: We must be ready for its consequences. And we will be ready."

In addition to his actions against Panama and Iraq, Bush kept his word by ordering the use of American jet fighters in the Philippines to quell a coup attempt against Corazon Aquino, by sending special forces to El Salvador after guerrillas seized a hotel where American military advisers were staying, and by dispatching military advisers to Colombia to aid that nation's war on drug cartels.

And while the world was transfixed with the gulf crisis, Bush dispatched Marines to rescue sixty-some Americans from revolution-torn Liberia and 260 others, including the U.S. and Soviet ambassadors, from troubled Somalia.

"Whether we will see further moves of this sort in the months and years ahead cannot, of course, be determined at this point,"

Klare wrote. "There is no question, however, that both the president's public statements and the Pentagon's formal military planning envision a more active U.S. military role in the Third World."

Not surprisingly, then, Bush seemed to thrive on his role as commander in chief during the Persian Gulf War, and was quick to thank returning troops for their "incredible acts of bravery" that had helped to build "a renewed sense of pride and confidence here at home." Thanks to their victory, he said, "The first test of the new world order has been passed" and "the specter of Vietnam has been buried forever in the desert sands of the Arabian Peninsula."

Fears of a civil war in the Soviet Union reportedly even had officials in the White House and Pentagon discussing contingency plans for intervention, particularly to protect the Baltic states from Soviet occupation.

George Black, an editor at the *Nation,* was one of the few observers at the height of the postwar euphoria to publicly question Bush's aggressive approach to international differences. Writing in the *Los Angeles Times,* Black observed that:

> One of the first lessons to emerge from the rubble of Kuwait is a surprising and paradoxical one: that America's wars are likely to enjoy broader public support if they are unencumbered by any pretense that the United States is fighting to defend democracy. Americans are more comfortable, it seems, with war as an assertion of naked power, designed not to make over foreign countries in our own image but to destroy and humiliate those to whom we have taken a dislike. . . .
>
> Much more satisfying than a war burdened by the hard sell of democracy is one in which absolute evil is vanquished by absolute good—embodied, by definition, in the Stars and Stripes. There was no sentimental nonsense about democracy in the review of national security policy that Bush ordered at

the start of his presidency. It simply advised: "In cases where the U.S. confronts much weaker enemies, our challenge will be not simply to defeat them, but to defeat them decisively and rapidly."

This also appears to involve a ritual of humiliation, in which the enemy is first vilified in a manner that recalls the daily Two Minutes Hate directed at the huge projected face of the traitor Goldstein in George Orwell's *1984*. . . . This extends from the respectable elite media—as in the *New Republic*'s embellishing a cover photo of Hussein to make his mustache resemble Hitler's—to the yahoo culture, with its Hussein dart boards, its Scudbuster T-shirts, and the electric chair in one New York store where customers have been paying $5 for the privilege of throwing the switch on the tacky Iraqi. . . .

From Truman to Reagan, every postwar U.S. president has cloaked his crusades in the language of democracy. Bush appears to prefer a more direct approach. One of the minor cultural artifacts of this war was a button that read, quoting the president, "America kicks butt." The question is, does it any longer know how to do anything else?

The answer, unfortunately, is that it may not have to. As the U.S. military humbled Hussein's alleged army, it was also showing off the latest high-tech American weapons to fascinated foreign buyers, who quickly got in line to take a closer look.

Among the countries expressing interest in the Patriot missile after its supposed success at stopping Scuds, were such freedom-loving nations as Turkey, South Korea, and Thailand, as well as Israel.

And Bush's best buddies, the British, appeared likely to get into the act by buying more than five hundred M-1A1 tanks, a high-tech marvel that won praise for its performance in the war. That kind of purchase would be a $1 billion boost to General Dynamics.

At the same time Bush called for "less proliferation of all kinds of weapons" in the wake of the war, he also said with a wink that no arms embargo would be allowed to threaten the security of America's friends.

All told, Bush had plans in the works to sell $18 billion in weapons to the war-wracked Mideast nations by 1992.

Even worse, he proposed that the federal Export-Import Bank underwrite arms sales to needier nations by backing up to $1 billion in bank loans to supplement already extant Pentagon loan guarantees.

And just eight months after forgiving Egypt's $6.8 billion in weapons-loan debts, Bush announced plans to sell the impoverished nation $1.6 billion in new weapons.

Part of the impetus for new arms sales in the explosive region was coming from defense contractors faced with a large reduction in U.S. spending for the rest of the decade. Without foreign orders for the M-1A1 tank, for example, General Dynamics might have to shut down its production lines in Michigan and Ohio before the late 1990s, when the Army plans to order a new battle tank.

Foreign sales also might be the only way for McDonnell-Douglas, Northrop, Lockheed, Grumman, and General Dynamics to keep their production lines open if the Pentagon doesn't come up with large new orders, which is considered unlikely.

In addition to the Persian Gulf states, other Third World nations were reported to be scouring the market for high-tech weapons—an estimated forty nations were seeking "stealth" technology alone—after seeing their apparent effectiveness against Iraq. They also said it was unfair for the United States and the Western powers that already had such weapons to now try to limit their purchase or development by others.

"To undermine the science, technology, research, and modern advances in defense is disastrous," said Prime Minister Nawaz Sharif of Pakistan in an address in which he stressed the need for Pakistan to become "an impregnable fortress."

This worries U.S. officials because it could end up leveling the playing field in future wars the United States might enter, and also because it ensures that future Third World wars will be more destructive.

The Soviet Union and China suddenly feel forced to put development of such weapons on the fast track, and are likely to sell them to other nations to help finance the required research and development.

Sen. John Glenn, D-Ohio, who has been warning against the folly of America's arms-sales policy for more than a decade, predicted just such postwar developments at the war's beginning.

"Let us harbor no illusions about the utility of military measures as a long-term solution to the problem of proliferation," Glenn wrote in the Senate publication *Proliferation Watch* at the height of the Persian Gulf War. He continued:

> Buildings, once flattened, can readily be rebuilt. Scientific knowledge is hard to bomb. Biological agents can be cultivated with little difficulty. The underlying political motivations that inspire nations to seek weapons of mass destruction are also best addressed by solutions. Similarly, the economic pressures and raw greed that motivated international suppliers of sensitive weapons-related technology will still be there after the smoke clears. . . .
>
> As we review our laws and work for improved international controls, we should do so with a sober realization—illuminated by recent events—that the cost of today's exports may be yet another war tomorrow.

But Glenn was assuming, of course, that having another war tomorrow is something the United States wants to avoid. If that's true, it will have to try a lot harder than it has in the recent past— especially in the volatile Middle East.

Unfortunately, if events are true to Mideast history, the war's effects will be felt for decades throughout the region and beyond.

Establishing Linkage

After going to war largely because of his refusal to link the Iraqi-Kuwaiti and Arab-Israeli disputes, the first and biggest challenge to Bush's "new world order" was to do exactly that.

Bush's extreme enforcement of U.N. Security Council resolutions requiring Hussein to quit Kuwait compared with his refusal to force Israel to comply with Resolution 242 of 1967, which demanded Israeli withdrawal from occupied Arab lands, increased the need to resolve the latter issue at the same time it made the task more difficult.

But the administration had no real choice but to try, because, as Mideast analyst Charles Snow wrote in the *Middle East Economic Survey,* a weekly oil-industry newsletter:

> Unless a new and very different peace is made . . . there's a real danger that the campaign to reverse Iraq's annexation of Kuwait will destroy the very interests it is intended to protect.
>
> If the war for Kuwait proves anything, it is that no one—Arab, European, American or even Israeli—can afford to leave the Middle East as it was before. . . . The next time regional instability precipitates a conflict—and there will be a next time unless all the causes of the present one are dealt with—it would lead to a catastrophe of truly global proportions.

Secretary of State Baker seemed to be attempting to translate this challenge into an opportunity when he testified to the House Foreign Affairs Committee on February 6.

"Let's not fool ourselves," he said. "The course of this crisis has stirred emotions among Israelis and Palestinians that will not yield easily to conciliation. Yet, in the aftermath of this war, as in earlier wars, there may be opportunities for peace—if the parties are willing."

On the same day, however, Jordan's King Hussein raised the concerns of many Arabs regarding America's real intentions.

"The talk about a new world order whose early feature is the destruction of Iraq . . . leads us to wonder about the identity of this order," he said in a speech that outraged Washington. "The real purpose behind this destructive war . . . is to destroy Iraq and rearrange the area [under U.S. domination]," he predicted.

Gen. Schwarzkopf's March 24 announcement that the United States was closer than ever to establishing a permanent military headquarters on Arab soil only added to the suspicions King Hussein expressed about America's true motives.

Such a headquarters would meet a longstanding American aim of having a land base in the Persian Gulf—a goal Arab governments have balked at for decades.

"There's a possibility we will be moving a forward headquarters element of Central Command—not the entirety . . . someplace over here on the gulf," the general told reporters. "But there's an awful lot of negotiations that have to go on, the locations have to be accepted and all the arrangements have to be made. . . . We're certainly much closer to that now than we've ever been before."

Elaborating on Schwarzkopf's remarks later, an American said the headquarters would be involved in planning and in communicating with various Mideast military forces.

Under this plan, the Central Command would be the major partner in an alliance built around the Arab allies that fought Iraq. Ideally, Arab ground forces would be backed by an enlarged U.S. naval force that would have greater access to Arab ports, as well as by regular deployments of U.S. fighter wings and ground troops for visits and exercises.

The headquarters' most likely location was said to be in Bahrain, where the U.S. and British air forces had maintained secret bases for several years. But the issue was a sensitive one. Before the war, Bahrain not only refused to acknowledge that the bases existed, but also insisted that the two Western governments keep secret their existence.

Two days after Schwarzkopf's "headquarters" bombshell, Gen. Peter de la Billiere, commander of the British forces, dropped another one when he announced that the allies planned to keep ground forces in Kuwait to guard against future Iraqi military incursions.

De la Billiere revealed before leaving the region on March 26 that he had asked that some British forces stay in Kuwait indefinitely after forces in Saudi Arabia and Iraq had been withdrawn.

U.S. officials said American forces would also remain in the region for an undisclosed period. They previously had discounted that possibility because the Kuwaiti government had been cool to the idea.

Some Arabs who had supported the U.S. intervention began having second thoughts after Schwarzkopf's March 24 announcement, and those who had opposed it were expressing outright outrage (Libyan leader Moammar Gadhafi, for example, charged that Bahrain would become "an American colony"). Meanwhile, most Israelis were staking out a position even more antithetical to resolving their dispute with Arabs of the occupied territories.

"There's no Left left in Israel," Daniel Levine, a professor at Israel's Bar Ilan University, told the author as the war was nearing its end. "The peace movement in Israel at this time is almost nonexistent. Iraq's unprovoked aggression on Israel radicalized almost everyone."

As an indication of that, the *New York Times* reported that at one point, after referring to veteran hard-liner Ariel Sharon, Israel Radio said, "and then to the right of him. . . ."

"When Sharon no longer defines the right edge of Israeli politics, it means there are some awfully angry Israelis," the *Times* said.

That certainly seemed to be the case when Israel's rightist government rejected President Bush's call for a solution to the

Israeli-Palestinian conflict that included trading occupied land for peace with Israel's Arab neighbors.

Even before Baker had a chance to present Bush's proposal, Prime Minister Yitzhak Shamir's government made it clear that a "new world order" envisioned by Bush wasn't welcome if it included the surrender of occupied territories.

"We have some problem with the very concept that . . . progress must mean territorial concessions," said Avi Pazner, the prime minister's spokesman. "Maybe there are other ways."

Foreign Minister David Levy was more blunt. "We disagree on this issue," he said.

A week after Baker returned from his Mideast tour, State Department spokesman Margaret Tutwiler said governments there "are doing some serious, genuine thinking" about Baker's proposals. She added, however, that "we're at a very early stage here."

Tutwiler then criticized Israel's decision to deport four Palestinian leaders from the occupied territories. The move "cannot possibly contribute to the development of a peace process," she said.

Noting that Baker had asked Shamir to consider taking incremental steps toward improving conditions for Palestinians in the occupied territories, Tutwiler said the deportations were "not exactly" the kind of steps Baker had in mind.

During his tour, Baker reportedly outlined specific steps each government could take to begin the peace process broached by Bush.

The 1967 U.N. resolutions Bush had said could serve as a basis for negotiations demanded Israel's pullout from land taken from Jordan, Egypt, and Syria, as well as the fixing of secure borders for all the area's nations, including Israel.

Israel did give the captured Sinai peninsula back to Egypt after reaching a U.S.-brokered accord in 1979. But Tel Aviv has legally annexed the strategically crucial Golan Heights, taken from

Syria in 1967, and has slowly increased its presence in the Gaza Strip, taken from Egypt, and the West Bank, taken from Jordan, where a combined 1.7 million Palestinians live.

The shaky status of Palestine Liberation Organization Chairman Yasser Arafat further complicates matters in the Mideast. At war's end, some Arabs considered Arafat a disloyal clown. But not the Palestinians, as they made clear to Baker during their meeting with him. If the Israelis want Arafat out of the picture, analysts say, they will have to prove to Palestinians that they will get a better deal without him.

But the Israelis weren't in a very generous mood after the war. And it didn't help matters that, in the first three-and-a-half weeks of "peace," more Israelis were killed by knife-wielding Palestinians from the occupied territories than by all of Iraq's Scud missiles.

That caused the Israeli government to consider banning all unmarried Palestinian men under age thirty from entering Israel to work, since most of the suspects in the stabbings fit that profile and were working legally in Israel.

Such a move would adversely affect the ability of thousands of Palestinians to earn a living, and further damage the territories' economies.

Adding fuel to the fire, as he usually does, Housing Minister Ariel Sharon announced "speeded up" plans to add thirteen thousand housing units to Israeli settlements in the West Bank during the next two years. Sharon said the settlements had been chosen with the twin goals of preventing Arab towns from becoming too large and commanding the strategic high ground that might prove crucial in wartime.

For good measure, Sharon also argued that Israel not only should refuse to negotiate with the PLO, but also should refuse to negotiate with any Palestinian delegation from the territories that supported the PLO.

Sharon's plan appeared to violate the spirit of Prime Minister Shamir's promise that none of the nearly half a billion dollars in loan guarantees the United States made for housing for Soviet immigrants would be used to build in the occupied territories. The Israeli government tried to get around that problem by saying the plan was the product of an individual ministry and therefore not official government policy.

The proposal obviously angered Arab leaders, who had expressed fears all along that Israel would try to put as many Soviet Jews as possible in the occupied territories before Arab-Israeli negotiations got started.

In contrast to the lack of criticism of Sharon's plan, when Israeli military chief of staff Lt. Gen. Dan Shomron suggested Israel might be better off giving up the occupied territories in return for peace, he earned the wrath of many officials.

Several times, Shamir has proposed giving the occupied territories a measure of autonomy as an interim step. But he won't say toward what, and the Palestinians don't seem to care, because mere autonomy doesn't interest them—only independence does.

By the end of Baker's first postwar Mideast mission, the U.S. land-for-peace proposal had been endorsed by eight Arab governments.

But Baker nonetheless rejected an Arab request for a Mideast peace conference.

"This is not the appropriate time," he said, adding that he did not make detailed recommendations to the Arab ministers on Israel because "it is early. We still have a long way to go."

Iran, as the new major power in the region, certainly would have agreed. Tehran by that point had its own plan for the region: the establishment of a fundamentalist-controlled bloc of states stretching from the Indian subcontinent right up to the the West Bank.

According to several reports, four days before Iranian President

Rafsanjani called for Hussein to "surrender to the will of the people" and promised to support the Shiite uprising in Iraq, the Iranian National Security Council agreed to begin aiding both the Shiite rebels in southern Iraq and the two Kurdish fighting movements in the north.

At the same time, Iran reportedly began aiding the Jordanian Islamic fundamentalist movement, with the goal of turning Jordan, too, into an Islamic republic.

Dirty Aftermath

Further complicating the future of the Mideast are the environmental damage caused by the war and the growing shortage of water, which is rapidly becoming more valuable than oil and could, in the future, cause conflicts every bit as bitter as those caused by oil.

Extinguishing the ferocious oil-well fires in Kuwait was proving to be a task of astounding proportions. And a shortage of funds wasn't helping matters.

"The magnitude of the problem is becoming greater every day," Kuwait's acting oil minister, Rasheed al-Amiri, said. "We think it will take one to two years to put out the fires, but no one really knows. It could be longer."

The burning wells were consuming an estimated six million barrels of oil—valued at more than $100 million—per day and pouring tons of toxic chemicals and soot into the air. The air was so bad in Kuwait City that at one point the U.N. Environmental Program believed the city might have to be evacuated.

At the same time, the oil slicks that stained the Persian Gulf during the war had fouled an estimated two hundred miles of Saudi Arabian coastline, from Kuwait in the north to Jubail in the south, according to a U.N. Environmental Program report.

In some parts of the gulf, the U.N. report said, there were "literally acres and acres of solid oil five to six inches deep."

The cleanup of the oil spill also was complicated by a shortage of money, but had at least succeeded in keeping the Saudi desalination plants open to produce precious fresh water.

Kuwait hadn't been so lucky, however. Iraqi forces destroyed or disabled most of the emirate's desalination facilities before fleeing in February.

While the oil-well fires and oil spills were gaining most of the attention of environmentalists and the media, Egyptian-born geologist Farouk El-Baz was worried about a more gritty issue: sand. El-Baz, the director of the Center for Remote Sensing at Boston University and an expert on Middle Eastern desert geology, warned that the widespread disruption of the desert surface might cause a doubling of sand storms and an encroachment of dunes on towns, farms, roads, and airports in Kuwait.

"As far as long-term damage, this is a more severe problem" than the spills or the fires, El-Baz told the *Baltimore Sun* in March.

In the March 8 issue of *Science* magazine, El-Baz wrote that the huge sand expanses in the Mideast are fragile, dynamic systems.

After its disruption during the war, he said, a new generation of sand dunes might begin moving south along the west side of the gulf as soon as the winds arrived in May. "The dunes can move quickly," El-Baz said. "This is a remarkably fluid environment that has no respect for what's in its way."

As for water, all you have to do is look at a map of the Mideast and study its weather and population trends to see why the issue is bound to boil over.

Populations are growing far faster than the area's aquifers can be restored. Rainfall in the region is as fleeting as it is fickle. And shrinking rivers are shared by nations already at odds.

Syria, for example, has begun damming the Euphrates and is diverting part of its decreasing volume, which would normally flow into Iraq.

Turkey has been doing the same thing further upstream.

Egypt has been increasingly at odds with the Sudan over the declining volume of water in the Nile.

Israel, Syria, and Jordan have all been draining the Jordan River at rising rates, and Israel's growing use of a large West Bank aquifer has been further increasing tensions in the area.

Add an Arab population growth rate of 3 percent a year and the deluge of Soviet immigrants to Israel, and you have a potential for conflict in a region that hardly needs another excuse to fight.

No wonder there was speculation that the White House was working to stifle rising concerns that the United States might be mired in a Middle East quagmire.

Those concerns were heightened when Colin Powell said troops might be in Iraq for some time to come. That caused some foreign governments to point out that the United States had no business interfering in internal Iraqi political affairs.

To allay fears of U.S. meddling, Bush told reporters in late March that it would be "inappropriate to try to shape or suggest even what government should follow on [after Hussein]. I would hope that it would be one that could work very compatibly with the Western powers, Western countries, and live happily ever after."

Unfortunately, the Mideast has never been a land of fairy tales come true.

That's why, writing in the *Los Angeles Daily News,* Marcus G. Raskin, a member of President Kennedy's National Security Council and co-director of the private Institute for Policy Studies, drew the following "harsh conclusions" from the allied intervention:

- First, . . . hundreds of thousands of people will die of starvation, war, and plague as major centers of Arab civilizations are destroyed.
- Second, the United States [will find] itself quietly sup-

porting Saddam and the Republican Guard as a counterpoise
to Iraqi anarchy as it seeks favor from another dictator, Hafez
Assad of Syria.

• Third, each nation will feel compelled to obtain more
arms because weapons are shown as "effective" instruments of
maintaining and securing power.

• Fourth, to please the United States, Saudi Arabia and
the gulf states will initiate sham democratic measures in order
to legitimize local oligarchic control.

• Fifth, the United States does not know what is in its
national interest in the Israel-Palestinian-Arab conflict. On the
other hand, it acts as an impartial bròker because all parties
view it as having interests that it refuses to disclose.

Expediential politicians seek immediate advantage irrespec-
tive of long-term consequences while the statesperson sees far,
seeking means to resolve longstanding injustice on all sides. It
is our unfolding political tragedy that we have many of the
former and very few of the latter.

If Raskin is right, Bush's brave new world order could collapse into a disorder from which it may take decades to recover.

Winners and Losers

George Bush definitely won the war of weapons in his high-noon desert duel with Saddam Hussein. But the high-pitched war of words between Bush and Hussein may have been—at best—a draw.

How could this be when hundreds of thousands of Hussein's own people turned against him while Bush's approval rating among Americans soared to record heights? Ask J. R. McLeod, an assistant professor of anthropology at Ohio State University.

In a paper presented at a conference on political rhetoric at the University of Iowa shortly after the war, McLeod contended that, despite his military defeat, Hussein had "managed to change the nature of the political rhetoric surrounding Middle Eastern issues." He continued:

> Whatever the outcome personally for Hussein, the world is now discussing the conflict between the rich and poor Arab nations; linkage concerning the extremely complex relationship that exists between the gulf crisis and the Palestinian question; and nations as far afield as Indonesia, Malaysia, Pakistan, and Singapore seriously debated whether or not the Gulf War was indeed a *jihad.*

From Algeria, which backed Hussein, to Tunisia, which did the same, to Jordan, where Saddam has become a cult icon, the nature of Arab rhetoric about themselves, their place in history, their conflict with the West, and their ultimate destiny in the family of nations has been placed on a completely different rhetorical plane. More people around the world are conscious of the powerful potential of pan-Arabism than ever before.

McLeod said the immense cultural differences between the Arab and Western worlds greatly contributed to the misunderstandings that caused the crisis and then escalated it.

This was exacerbated by the first-ever use of satellite television by each leader to bypass the other and speak directly to the adversary nation's citizens. This approach could have merit. But it failed miserably in this instance because Bush and Hussein each tried to convert his audience without adjusting his rhetorical style.

As a result, misunderstandings were enlarged rather than reduced. Eventually, McLeod says, Bush and Hussein "had boxed themselves into their rhetorical corners from which the only face-saving option was a shooting war."

Both the Arab and Western worlds could and should learn from this failure to communicate. It's not the first time the problem has come up, McLeod says, and it won't be the last if the citizens of different nations don't do a better job of reading one another's lips.

One thing the West can do is try to understand the origins and purposes of the provocative prose of a Saddam Hussein as evidenced by his talk of "burning the bodies of the corrupt and evil invaders" and his threat to make the ground war "a hellfire that will sear their scoundrels."

Such hyperbole, McLeod notes, comes from the classical Arabic of the Koran. Arab speeches that draw on this, Peter Mansfield explains in his book, *The Arabs,* "are magnificent in sound and color. They achieve their effect through the use of all the vast linguistic resources of the language: emphasis, exaggeration, elaborate metaphor, and even a form of *saj,* a classical type of rhymed prose for which Arabic is ideally suited. The result is a semipoetic rhetoric which can be highly intoxicating, sweeping the listeners along on a current of words."

Unfortunately, a lot gets lost in the translation. As a consequence, McLeod says, even though Saddam successfully "raised the rhetorical ante on the Middle East as few Arab leaders have ever done in history," he did so at great cost.

That, he adds, fulfilled Mansfield's warning about the dangers of the hyperbole of Arab rhetoric: "This Arab trait has been an incalculable drawback for the nation in the struggle for unity and independence in modern times. On countless occasions the Arabs have been led by their own rhetoric to believe that they were about to achieve their aspirations. They have woken to reality with a hangover which lasted until the next bout of self-justification."

April Fools

But self-justification became popular in postwar Washington, too, when U.S. Ambassador April Glaspie broke an eight-month silence March 20 and gave her version of her controversial meeting with Hussein—a meeting to which, *Newsweek* reported, she conveniently neglected to take the customary notetaker. Appearing at an informal hearing of the Senate Foreign Relations Committee as an unsworn witness, Glaspie insisted that Hussein had assured her he would not attack Kuwait after she forcefully warned him that the United States "would defend our vital interests, we would support the right of self-defense of our friends in the gulf."

Her account greatly contradicted the transcript of the meeting released by Baghdad in September, which quoted Glaspie as telling

Hussein that the United States had "no opinion on the Arab-Arab conflicts, like your border disagreement with Kuwait."

Glaspie described the "so-called transcript" as "disinformation . . . edited to the point of inaccuracy." To hear Glaspie tell it, she had a dictator previously portrayed by the Bush administration as a fearless, ruthless, murderous megalomanic virtually eating out of her hand.

"He, I think, felt stymied," she said. "He surrendered. . . . He wanted me to inform President Bush that he would not solve his problems with Kuwait by violence, period. . . . It was a strange atmosphere because he was conciliatory and he normally is not."

Although she spoke repeatedly of Hussein's long record for duplicity, Glaspie said she took Hussein at his word. She left for vacation five days later, even though there were a hundred thousand Iraqi troops massed on the Kuwait border. Three days later, those troops overran Kuwait.

One of the few senators with the temerity to challenge the tough-talking career diplomat asked whether the Bush administration had misjudged Hussein.

"Our mistake was that, like every other government in the world, we foolishly did not realize that he was stupid," Glaspie replied. "He did not believe our clear and repeated warnings."

Adding to the problem, she said, was the Mideast's history of minor border incursions (which many believe the United States was prepared to accept in this instance). It also perplexed Glaspie that Iraq seemed to be on the verge of getting concessions from Kuwait without firing a shot.

She described Hussein's decision to invade as "a passing fancy" and "an extraordinary miscalculation." His biggest miscalculation, she said, was that the other gulf nations wouldn't allow U.S. troops into the region.

Glaspie explained away her her eight-month silence by saying,

"It simply seemed it was not a time for retrospectives. It was a time to build our forces and to build the coalition."

She also said she had acted on the instructions of Washington when she sent a letter to Iraqi Foreign Minister Tariq Aziz that apologized for a "Voice of America" criticism of Hussein. She said Washington feared the editorial might have been interpreted as an incitement to revolution.

Although Glaspie's testimony was full of contradictions and raised numerous questions, the deferential senators seemed more interested in praising Glaspie than in interrogating her.

That delighted the White House. "She did great," said presidential spokesman Marlin Fitzwater. "The truth will out."

And to a certain extent it did, the next day—but not quite the way the White House had expected. Glaspie wasn't about to get by with another spring snow job during her appearance before the House Foreign Affairs Middle East subcommittee. Not with the subcommittee's hard-charging chairman, Indiana Democrat Lee Hamilton, running the show. After putting Glaspie through nearly four hours of tough questioning, Hamilton pointed out that the administration had ignored a series of signs that Iraq was becoming more bellicose in the months before its invasion of Kuwait.

"I get the impression that no one in the high levels of policymaking at the State Department was paying much attention to Iraq until the end of July 1990," he told Glaspie. "I get the impression that during those six or eight months prior to August 2, Iraq's policy changed, and changed in a very negative way toward the United States. But U.S. policy did not change. The warning bells went off, but nobody in Washington was listening."

Hamilton cited several conflicting statements from U.S. officials—including those of State Department spokeswoman Margaret Tutwiler and Assistant Secretary of State John Kelly that the United States had "no special defense or security commitments to Kuwait." He also pointed out that the administration was fighting congressional moves to slap economic sanctions on Iraq.

"It is a record which confused me, confused this subcommittee . . . and it is not unreasonable to think it might have confused Saddam Hussein as well," Hamilton told Glaspie.

"There was no doubt in my mind that he knew we meant business," she snapped back.

But then Tom Lantos, a California Democrat, told the ambassador he was "appalled by the frighteningly flawed judgment" she displayed.

Noting that "very few people were sure we would move militarily, on this committee or in this country," Lantos told Glaspie, "I think you need to have a very high dose of humility, in retrospect."

Rep. Stephen Solarz, a Vietnam dove turned Persian Gulf hawk, asked if the committee could see the account of the meeting that Glaspie cabled to Washington, but she claimed that releasing the document would set a precedent that would have a chilling effect on diplomacy.

More than a few observers found Glaspie's position bogus at best. In 1943, for example, the State Department released an 895-page volume on U.S. policies leading to Pearl Harbor. *Peace and War: United States Foreign Policy, 1931-1941* included numerous confidential diplomatic cables on the most sensitive matters of the era, and remains an important source on the origins of World War II.

So why was the State Department so adamant about not releasing the cable?

According to the *New York Times* columnist William Safire, Glaspie's internal "memcon" of the meeting "confirmed the wimpishness suggested by the transcript."

Besides, Safire wondered, "If our envoy was so blameless, why had she been left to twist in the wind while Assistant Secretary

John Kelly and his Near East cohort [whom Safire did not name] said the transcript was essentially accurate?"

Noting that there was no love lost between Kelly and Glaspie, Safire said Kelly "gleefully drove her into the bureaucratic wilderness as a scapegoat."

Unfortunately, Safire continued, "The lady knew too much. If not rehabilitated, she could spill the beans about Kelly's February 12, 1990, visit to Baghdad, records of which he is desperately trying to deep-six. (If the Glaspie memcon is released, the Kelly memcon must follow; one dead hand washes the other.) That's why our State Department is closing ranks, cooking up strange stories about protecting the nation from distractions."

So despite Glaspie's beautifully scripted performance, too many questions remained for her to come out a winner.

Guess Whose Son Won?

One minor figure who came out a winner in a major way, according to the April issue of *Common Cause* magazine, was George W. Bush, the president's oldest son.

Thirty years after Zapata Offshore Oil, a Texas company George Bush helped to found, drilled the first well in the Persian Gulf off Kuwait, George W. Bush was the third-largest insider stockholder in another Texas oil company that obtained offshore drilling rights in the Persian Gulf, this time off Bahrain.

Common Cause quoted reports filed by the Harken Energy Corporation with the Securities and Exchange Commission as saying the younger Bush's company had obtained the "exclusive right to explore for, develop and produce petroleum throughout substantially all of Bahrain's offshore territories."

The quick ending to the war gave Harken a chance to fulfill its requirement to drill an exploratory well by January 30, 1992.

Having a first-ever permanent U.S. military base in Bahrain and closer ties between the two nations wouldn't hurt, either.

So Bush's son was a big winner. But almost everyone's standing paled in comparison with the military's new status. In the spring of 1990, 18 percent of the people polled by the Times Mirror Center for the People and the Press gave the military a "very favorable" rating. A year later, that figure had more than tripled. Gen. H. Norman Schwarzkopf, Operation Desert Storm's commander, received a very favorable rating of 62 percent, the highest by far in the poll's history. The previous record-high rating among leaders of the present and recent past—39 percent for the late President John F. Kennedy, recorded in the spring of 1987—also was surpassed by Gen. Colin Powell: Fifty-one percent of those surveyed were disposed "very favorably" to the chairman of the Joint Chiefs of Staff.

Even the the much-maligned Congress and its Democratic leaders came out ahead. In the spring of 1990, only 6 percent of the survey's respondents gave Congress a very favorable rating; a year later, 16 percent did. House Speaker Thomas S. Foley's "very favorable" rating jumped from 3 percent to 13 percent, and House Majority Leader Richard Gephardt's rose 3 percent to 11 percent.

A more surprising winner in the war was the long-pilloried press. After complaining about coverage of the Persian Gulf War and supporting as much censorship as the military wished to apply, a surprising 59 percent of Americans in a *Newsweek* poll said they thought better of the press after the war than they did before.

A similar NBC survey found that 40 percent of Americans said coverage of the war had left them with greater—rather than less—respect for the media. Only 20 percent said the opposite. And a *Los Angeles Times* poll showed that 62 percent of the people found the news media "unbiased" in their war coverage.

"There's no question that there's a euphoria that has much

to do with the approval for everybody," Donald S. Kellermann, who directed the survey, told the Associated Press. "It's very much like a football game. The blood lust is up and when you win, the blood lust is satisfied. It's the 'We're No. 1' feeling."

So the media's popularity shouldn't have been too surprising afterall. But one of its suddenly vocal fans was. He was Army Lt. Gen. Thomas Kelly, the sometimes-testy, sometimes-genial general who battled with reporters daily in televised briefings during Operation Desert Storm. After disarming the nation with a charming combination of bluntness, humor, and believability, Kelly finally disarmed the press, too, when, after announcing his retirement during his final briefing on March 4, the 58-year-old Kelly saluted reporters and scolded the public for criticizing them.

"I got a lot of letters from people who really don't understand the hurly-burly and give-and-take of a press briefing," Kelly said. "At no time were you ever impolite to me and at no time did I ever become offended. As you know, I hold a lot of you in great respect.

"Having a free press has served the United States well for 215 years," he added. "It is a crucial element in our democracy, and if anybody needs a contrast, all they have to do is look at the country that didn't have a free press and see what happened there." (One reason for Kelly's good mood might have been that *he* certainly came out of the war a winner. When he entered retirement April 1, he reportedly had about fifty speeches lined up, at about $20,000 apiece.)

Even President Bush had some nice things to say about journalists when he spoke at the Radio and Television Correspondents' Association dinner on March 19.

Bush said the war had "reminded us of the value of a free press," and he offered a toast "to the men and women who are the eyes and the ears of democracy."

On a more humorous note, Bush said he was urged to take

the Desert Storm coalition all the way to Baghdad to "take out the man who caused so much grief and anger. And I said, no, let CNN take Peter Arnett out."

Three weeks later, Arnett received a hero's welcome at the National Press Club, where he calmly defended his reporting from Baghdad.

Arnett, a Pulitzer Prize–winning news veteran of seventeen wars, said he had guarded his credibility carefully in Iraq by insisting on being allowed a spontaneous discussion with CNN anchors back in the States, after each approved and scripted broadcast. He convinced Iraqi officials that if he was perceived as having no freedom, his reports would have no influence.

"I think that helped enormously to reduce fears that I was some kind of robot reading what I was forced to write," he said.

Arnett said he was surprised by Sen. Alan Simpson's attack on him as an Iraqi "sympathizer," and noted that just a year before, theWyoming Republican had criticized Arnett and other reporters in Jerusalem for being too hard on Hussein when the Bush administration was seeking better ties with the dictator. Although the earlier story on Simpson's criticisms never ran on CNN, Arnett added that "we do still have the video, Senator."

Knowing full well his slander of the engaging, self-effacing Arnett wasn't wearing well, Simpson apologized—sort of—for his false allegation that Arnett's Vietnamese wife had a brother active in the Viet Cong.

"I greatly regret any hurt, pain, or anguish that I have caused his family," Simpson wrote in a letter to the *New York Times*. "Just as Operation Desert Storm has healed many wounds left from Vietnam—it is also time to allow that wound to heal."

But Simpson then went on to repeat most of his other allegations. He labeled Arnett's war reporting "repugnant" and charged that his "tone and manner . . . was helpful to the government of Iraq and harmful to the United States."

Simpson concluded his letter by saying: "My choice of the word 'sympathizer' was not a good one. I wish I could have snatched it back and rephrased my remarks. The word 'dupe' or 'tool' of the Iraqi government would have been more in context with my original comments. However, I do know when I am wrong and stubborn—and for that I apologize."

With apologies like that, who needs attacks? Not Arnett. But it didn't matter a whole lot anyway. The more Simpson talked, the more foolish he sounded and the better Arnett and his colleagues appeared.

The easiest explanation of the news media's newfound respect was that they had the good fortune of reporting on a war that was a stunning success for the United States and its allies. Reporting what, given the bloody alternative, turned out to be good news put the media in a rare positive light.

Another, less likely, explanation was that Americans came to appreciate the journalists' professionalism and to understand that reporters often had to ask what seemed to be impertinent questions in order to get a straight answer.

A third explanation may be closer to the mark: Many news organizations, especially the television networks, simply surrendered to the Pentagon's restrictions and the public's euphoria.

With such overwhelming public approval for the war, Americans were not going to let the press whine its way into breaking the Pentagon's grip on news coverage. Doing so would have suggested disloyalty. Yet if the media had been able to do it, the public might have been less "loyal" too.

In retrospect, the Pentagon's plan to control the media worked beautifully for several reasons.

For one thing, censorship by "security review" ended up being concerned more with image than security. Profanity, over-descriptive language, or anything deemed embarrassing to the wholesome military image was deleted.

More important, security review forced pool reporters in the field to totally surrender control of their stories to the military for review and transmission to the military press headquarters in Dhahran, Saudi Arabia, where virtually all reports were needlessly delayed, often for two or three days, for petty reasons.

The combination of control of both the journalists in the field and their output resulted in the transmission of virtually no images of wounded or dead American soldiers, and only a few of the thousands of Iraqis killed in combat.

Briefings, from whence most of the news came, also worked to the Pentagon's distinct advantage. The attitude of most of those giving the briefings was exhibited by an Air Force officer, who, according to the *New York Times,* began his briefing with this greeting: "I'm not a great fan of the press and I want you to know where we stand with each other. I suppose the press has its purpose. But one thing is certain: You can't do me any good and you sure as hell can do me harm."

With officers like that in control, it shouldn't be surprising that briefings often took on the atmosphere of a cat-and-mouse game that played right into the public's perception that reporters are pushy fools and the officers are dedicated dispensers of the truth.

That's why much of the best war reporting came from those who circumvented the Pentagon's restrictive pool system and tedious briefings. One such reporter was retired Army Col. David Hackworth, the nation's most decorated living veteran, who covered the war for *Newsweek.*

In a retrospective at the end of the war, Hackworth had a few critical comments about the press, but was far more displeased "with the military's paranoia and their thought-police who control the press. Although I managed to go out on my own, we didn't have the freedom of movement to make an independent assessment of what the military is all about. Everything was spoon-fed. We were like animals in a zoo, and the press officers were the zookeepers who threw us a piece of meat occasionally."

Tellingly, Hackworth added, "I had more guns pointed at me by Americans and Saudis who were into controlling the press than in all my years of actual combat."

Philip Caputo, a war-correspondent-turned-best-selling-novelist, said that though he supported the war, "The Pentagon has been censoring the press beyond reasonable needs for military security, making sure we see only what it wants us to see, which is a war weirdly sanitized of the pain, fear, and death that are the essence of war."

The reason the Pentagon wanted it that way was simple: If Americans ever saw the full fury of war, they might be less inclined to support it. At least that was reportedly a fear of Bush and many of his top aides, who felt that, because of the Vietnam syndrome, Americans might not support another war fought halfway around the world for unclear objectives. So they captured the press and forced it to disseminate official, casualty-free news.

In every way possible, the Pentagon set out to limit the emotional impact of war on the American people. And it succeeded so well that many people decided they liked the media (and war) after all.

That's too bad. Because the last thing the media should want is to be popular for doing a lousy job.

And in informing the public by communicating important facts—which is what journalism is all about—television, America's main source of information, did a miserable job. Or so a random survey of 250 people in the Denver metropolitan area would seem to indicate.

After six months of increasing coverage of the Persian Gulf crisis, a University of Massachusetts survey conducted in February found that television viewers remained incredibly ill-informed. And the more they watched television, the less they knew.

Among viewers who watched less than an hour and a half a day, 16 percent thought Kuwait was a democracy, 22 percent knew of the Palestinian *intifada* against Israeli occupation of the West Bank and Gaza Strip, and 40 percent were aware that Iraq wasn't the only country to occupy another in the Mideast. Among heavy viewers (more than three hours a night), on the other hand, 32 percent thought Kuwait was a democracy, just 10 percent had heard of the *intifada,* and 23 percent were aware of occupations other than Iraq's.

Only 2 percent could identify Kuwaiti's lowering of oil prices as the immediate cause of the Iraqi invasion and fewer than a third knew that Israel was illegally occupying territories and part of Lebanon.

Most important, the survey found a direct link between knowledge of the situation and opposition to the war. Those who supported the war were twice as likely to falsely believe Kuwait was a democracy, and less than half as likely to know that before August 2, the official U.S. position on an Iraqi invasion was unclear. The only thing about which the war supporters were *more* knowledgeable was the name of the allegedly successful Patriot missile— which all goes to show that ignorance is more than mere bliss in America. It's also what passes for patriotism.

At any rate, if the news media think a few kind words from the Pentagon and the president and a few positive polls are going to change things in the future, they should take a close look at what Bush said in papers filed after the war with the court hearing the news media's suit against Pentagon censorship. "The commander-in-chief and his subordinates concluded that news coverage procedures which may have worked in the 1960s and the 1970s in Vietnam cannot work in the 1990s, with its explosion of media representatives, 'real-time' satellite transmissions, and high-technology warfare. . . . It is probable that, given the number of journalists who will desire to cover any future hostilities, [the

Department of Defense] will be forced to regulate access to U.S. troops and combat operations," he declared.

In a column, *Newsday*'s Sydney Schanberg, one of the leading plaintiffs in the suit, translated Bush's statement thus: "We the government have successfully established a precedent for information control, so if you in the press thought you were shackled during the Iraq war and blocked from access to the combat troops in forward areas and followed everywhere by Pentagon 'minders' and reduced to being rewriters of government communiques, you ain't seen nothin' yet. Wait till the next war."

The government made it clear it would prefer to wait till then to litigate the issue, too. It argued in a New York federal court that the journalists' suit should be dismissed because the Gulf War was over.

"The case is moot," Justice Department attorney Neil Koslowe said as he urged U.S. District Judge Leonard B. Sand of Manhattan to throw the case out of court.

The plaintiffs, however, argued that the case should go forward so the Pentagon would be prevented from hampering coverage of future wars.

Both sides were cool to Sand's proposal that the suit be tabled while the two sides review news coverage of the Persian Gulf War and try to devise a compromise on the Pentagon's restrictions.

Speaking for the news organizations, Franklin Siegel of the Center for Constitutional Rights said such discussions would be a waste of time because the military had tightened news-coverage restrictions after the 1983 invasion of Grenada and the 1989 invasion of Panama.

Sand said he was disappointed that the Pentagon refused to discuss an out-of-court settlement, and reserved decision on the government's motion for dismissal.

But the news media were the clear losers in another suit filed against military restrictions, when a federal judge in Washington,

D.C., refused to order the military to permit public and press access to the arrival of coffins of the war dead at Dover Air Force Base in Delaware.

"I can't substitute my judgment for that of the military," U.S. District Judge Royce C. Lamberth, who had served as an Army legal officer in Vietnam, said in refusing to issue a preliminary injunction ordering such access.

The plaintiffs—journalists, veterans, and a military family support group—argued that the policy was an unconstitutional effort to manipulate public opinion by not allowing the war's cost to sink into the public's consciousness.

Government attorney David Anderson argued that access to the base could interfere with its mission to support forces overseas, although that had never happened in the past.

Kate Martin, an attorney for the American Civil Liberties Union, said the decision would be appealed.

"Armsageddon"

Perhaps the biggest winners of all in the Persian Gulf War were the defense contractors who provided all the high-tech, razzle-dazzle weaponry that so mesmerized Americans that they never noticed most of the weapons weren't nearly as successful as portrayed.

While Pentagon briefings were dominated by reports on the 90-percent-accurate (or so the military maintained) smart bombs, it wasn't until well after the war's end that the Air Force said that smart bombs had made up barely 7 percent of the U.S. explosives dropped on Iraqi targets. The Air Force reluctantly disclosed that of the rest—presumably "dumb" bombs—70 percent had missed their targets. That could have made for a lot of "collateral damage," but we'll probably never really know.

Equally misleading was the precision portrayed in every videotape released by the Pentagon. Senior officers privately admitted they had viewed extensive footage of bombs that missed targets—or hit the wrong targets—but U.S. authorities released none of that film. The British military, after much prodding by the press, showed one video of a not-so-smart bomb going awry.

Those disturbing facts came out almost by mistake when Air Force Chief of Staff Mirrill A. McPeak made his first major postwar appearance, "to tell an American success story" and claim most of the credit for the easy defeat of Iraqi forces in Kuwait.

It was hardly coincidental that the Air Force chose the day of McPeak's brag-fest to release a 22-page paper making the case for the proposed C-17, the futuristic transport plane whose rising cost estimates had caused growing concern in Congress but that was given a better chance of approval in the postwar euphoria.

That kind of turnaround on weapons caused the Congressional Budget Office to warn that the savings from the Pentagon's planned troop cuts could be more than wiped out by a new generation of expensive weapons that would add more than $40 billion a year to defense spending.

Robert F. Hale of the CBO told a House committee that even if the Bush administration reduces the armed forces by 25 percent, the level of defense spending it has proposed for fiscal 1995 "will not be enough to support the smaller forces in the long run."

He pointed to the B-2 stealth bomber (the most expensive plane in history at a cost predicted to go as high as $1 billion each), the C-17 transport plane being pushed by McPeak, the SSN-21 attack submarine, the Advanced Tactical Fighter, and several others. And renewed interest in the Strategic Defense Initiative, boosted by the Patriot missile's great public-relations job, would add billions more.

But the U.S. defense industry isn't putting all its eggs in its American basket. "Foreign military sales are the only game in town right now," an American aerospace executive was quoted as saying by *Newsweek*.

And their favorite target apparently was going to be the region that needed weapons about as much as it needed a new fanatical religious sect.

"The next big push in the defense industry will be to exploit the Middle East," one upbeat lobbyist told *Newsweek* after a March meeting of advocates for the largest defense contractors. "This is not arms control. This is an arms opportunity."

It also could be an Armageddon opportunity, but that never seems to cross the minds of arms merchants.

The biggest winners among those arms-hungry Mideast nations were Egypt and Syria. The big losers were Iraq, of course, already impoverished Jordan, and the Palestine Liberation Organization.

In fact, Egypt, the largest and most influential Arab nation, made out like a bandit. It was forgiven a full quarter of its debts as the United States wrote off almost $7 billion; the wealthy gulf states canceled $7 billion; and the Group of Seven industrial nations said they were forgiving a third of an undisclosed amount owed them by Egypt. Cairo also earned pledges and grants of $3 billion. That made Egypt's net gain substantial, even after subtracting war costs and Suez Canal losses.

Egypt's political pluses were substantial, too. But they were nothing like Syria's. Before Iraq invaded Kuwait, President Hafez Assad was an international pariah. Eight months later, he was the most sought-after man in the Mideast, by diplomats and arms dealers alike.

With the United States agreeing to look the other way, Assad crushed the sixteen-year civil war in Lebanon and established a puppet government there. In the war's aftermath, Assad also was in a political position to play a pivotal part in any peace settlement or political restructuring of the Middle East.

Syria's sinking economy also was thrown a life preserver.

Officials visiting Damascus after the war bore gifts in the form of aid pledges totaling $5 billion. The European Community also lifted economic sanctions against Syria, and Britain restored diplomatic relations with Assad's government in November.

Did that mean Britain suddenly trusted Assad?

"Oh, no . . . no, indeed," Sir Anthony Acland, the British ambassador to the United States, told the author. "We have to watch his every step." One hopes they do so more closely than Britain and the United States watched their former friend Hussein.

Amin Gemayel, the former president of Lebanon, warned in an April 5 speech at the University of Michigan that trusting Assad was dangerous. Gemayel said bitterly that since Syria had taken control of Lebanon the previous October, it had turned it into a narcotics trafficking center.

Gemayel was echoing accusations made by many of Syria's Lebanese opponents that Assad had supported political factions that bought arms and power through a protected heroin industry in the Bekaa Valley.

Gemayel also said Syria was pretending to be involved in peace talks not because it supported them, but "because it remains opposed to any progress . . . and it is once again the principal threat to Israel."

The decision by the six Arab states of the Persian Gulf to suspend hundreds of millions of dollars in aid to Jordan and the PLO made clear two of the losers.

The new policy is one of "no forgiveness, no forgetting," according to Kuwait's Abdullah Bishara, secretary general of the Gulf Cooperation Council, a policy-making organization of the wealthy oil-producing states.

"How can you justify a continuing of aid to a country that turned its back on you?" Bishara said of King Hussein's Jordan. "There is no forgiveness for this. It is not a romance where lovers quarrel. The crime is too big to forgive."

PLO Chairman Yasser Arafat got a similar tongue-lashing. "Mr. Arafat took a very reckless course of action and will have to bear the consequences," Bishara said.

Until 1989, Jordan received about $200 million a year from Saudi Arabia alone, and the PLO received about $100 million a year from the gulf council states.

President Bush symbolically formalized the war's winning and losing nations on April 10, when he signed an emergency aid bill compensating Israel and Turkey for costs supposedly borne in the war and giving him the authority to withhold aid from Jordan. The bill funneled $650 million to Israel and $200 million to Turkey.

Perhaps the biggest losers of all in this are those who usually lose—the masses. And defeat and dejection are hardly what the Arab world needs.

The Arab population of 465 million is growing by 3.2 percent a year, and is expected to double in thirty years. The Persian Gulf War exacerbated tensions between the wealthy Arab oil states of the Persian Gulf and the poor Arab states, like Jordan, Algeria, Yemen, and Sudan.

Meanwhile, as the formal cease-fire ending the war took effect on April 12, chaos seemed to reign in Iraq, and the impression that the Persian Gulf crisis was far from over was growing.

"What we have now is worse than what we had when Iraq was in Kuwait," Christine Moss Helms, an Iraq scholar who has advised both the White House and the Pentagon during the crisis, told the *New York Times.* "We have a situation where we entered the region to put down the Iraqi threat, and we spent $80 to $100 billion to do it, we ejected the Iraqis from Kuwait, but what did we get for it? We still don't have Saddam Hussein out of power, and now we have this deteriorating situation on the frontier between the Persians, the Arabs, and the Turks."

Helms and many other Mideast experts said the U.S.-led coalition had destroyed so much of Iraq that it sparked a premature uprising that was doomed to failure. As a result, the United States faced leaving behind more than 60,000 Iraqi POWs and 25,000 civilian and military refugees in the American occupation zone, as well as millions of displaced Kurds who had rebelled after receiving U.S. moral (but not material) support, to ultimately face Hussein's wrath.

"This is the chaos that occurs in war, particularly when there is a civil war going on simultaneously," a senior military official told the *Los Angeles Times*. "After we leave, we are under no obligation to them."

So welcome, citizens, to the brave new world order where war is almost heaven—and peace is pure hell.

Epilogue

At this writing, more than three months after the Persian Gulf War supposedly ended, the death, destruction, dislocation, and destabilization it caused continues.

If a Harvard University prediction—that up to 170,000 Iraqi children will die in the next year from disease and lack of medical treatment resulting from the war—proves accurate, Desert Storm's death toll would reach 370,000 people, most of them innocent pawns on an international chessboard that still contains the supposedly vanquished Saddam Hussein.

At the same time, the United States is still finding it difficult to withdraw from northern Iraq, where troops are protecting Kurds driven from their homes by Iraqi forces battling Kurdish rebels. On May 24, a detachment of U.S. troops had to enter the strategic city of Dohuk in an attempt to coax the Kurds to return. Most have, but they are pleading for a long-term American presence to protect them from Hussein's troops. Still waiting to return are a much-overlooked million other Kurds living in squalid refugee camps across the border in Iran.

In the rest of Iraq, Hussein is amazing observers with the speed at which he is rebuilding vital facilities and restoring services.

On June 9, he also took another step at regaining popularity by canceling wartime labor laws imposed in 1980 and renewing pledges to open the political system to greater freedoms. On the same day, Iraq's much-vilified defender during the war, King Hussein of Jordan, signed an agreement with activists to revive a multiparty democracy thirty-four years after political parties were banned.

"Liberated" Kuwait, meanwhile, remains an environmental nightmare ruled by a maniacal monarchy so intent on revenge against alleged colloborators during the Iraqi occupation that it sentenced a man to fifteen years in prison for wearing a Saddam Hussein T-shirt. Then, on the same day Hussein was promising more political freedom in Iraq, a five-judge panel in Kuwait was imposing the first death sentence on a defendant accused of colloborating with Iraqi troops. The bewildered stateless man was never even afforded the opportunity to talk with his court-appointed attorney. No evidence was presented orally; no witnesses were called. And the prosecutor said the same fate undoubtedly awaits many of the three hundred others to stand "trial."

In the meantime, Hafez Assad of Syria has formalized by treaty his relatively peaceful takeover of Lebanon without any of the grief Hussein gained for his violent takeover of Kuwait. Maybe Hussein will live and learn. Then again, he might not live to learn if Bush continues to insist that the embargo against war-ravaged Iraq remain in effect until Hussein is toppled.

Intransigent Israel persists in its resistance to serious peace talks. It also persists in bombing Palestinian bases, with the excuse that Syrian control of Lebanon will lead to more guerrilla attacks. In three days in early June alone, the Israelis killed twenty-two people and wounded another eighty-two.

"We live in great days in Israel, . . . days in which air force jets strike and leave dead . . . the terrorists in Lebanon," former-terrorist-turned-prime-minister Yitzhak Shamir boasts.

The United States, of course, denounces the attacks, then

proceeds with its promise to give Israel a $700 million bonus in
military aid and ten F-15 fighter planes for staying out of the
war. Otherwise, it contents itself with expensive parades and talk
of more grand victories over Third World forces to come—because,
officials say, the threat of American military power may not be
enough to prevent its use.

"In the new era, we are the ones who can deter," Gen. Colin
Powell told the *Washington Post.* "We have overwhelming power,
and we have demonstrated the willingness to use it."

The popular chairman of the Joint Chiefs of Staff apparently
hasn't come to appreciate Paul Kennedy's wise warning in *The
Rise and Fall of the Great Powers* "that the United States now
runs the risk, so familiar to historians of the rise and fall of previous
great powers, of . . . 'imperial overstretch.' "

As for the news media, they are tried and found wanting in
many quarters, especially their own. Walter Goodman of the *New
York Times* complained in the *Columbia Journalism Review,* for
example, that "the military effectively shaped coverage from the
beginning to the end of the Gulf War. That encouraged the natural
wartime disposition to celebrate Our Brave Men and Women and
[to] censure, or even censor, anyone who didn't pitch in heartily
enough."

In the same publication, Laurie Garrett of *Newsday* told of
viewing the unedited feeds from the Baghdad bomb shelter devastated by American bombs. "They showed scenes of incredible
carnage," she wrote. "Nearly all the bodies were charred into
blackness; in some cases the heat had been so great that entire
limbs were burned off. Among the corpses were those of at least
six babies and ten children, most of them so severely burned that
their gender could not be determined. Rescue workers collapsed
in grief, dropping corpses; some rescuers vomited from the stench
of the still-smoldering bodies. . . .

"One can only wonder," Garrett continues, "how U.S. viewers

would have reacted if they had seen the unedited video, or at least more than the sanitized few moments that were aired."

But, of course, they never did.

Which is one of the many reasons that *The Nation* properly concluded that the main problem with the war coverage was with the media, not the government. "Self-censorship, self-deception, unexamined bias and just plain cowardice subverted the facts, obscured history and occluded criticism better than any imposed regime could have done," the magazine said in an editorial.

It also noted that when a photographer working for NBC supplied the network with the kind of footage described by Garrett, it not only didn't run the tape, it fired the photographer.

And that, multiplied many times over, is largely how Bush's deviously devised Desert Mirage came to be viewed as the thunderously triumphant Desert Storm.

Peace.